MAKING
MIRACLES

MAKING MIRACLES

Create New Realities
for Your Life and Our World

LYNN WOODLAND

namaste
PUBLISHING

Vancouver, Canada

NAMASTE PUBLISHING
Vancouver, Canada

Copyright 2011 by Lynn Woodland
First Printing 2011

Library and Archives Canada Cataloguing in Publication

Woodland, Lynn
    Making miracles : create new realities for your life and our
world / Lynn Woodland.

ISBN 978-1-897238-62-2

    1. New Thought. 2. Miracles. 3. Self-help techniques. I. Title.

BF639.W66 2011   299'.93   C2011-905737-9

Previously published as Holding A Butterfly, 40shades music &
publishing, 2011 (ISBN 978-1450742566)

Published by Namaste Publishing
P.O. Box 62084
Vancouver, BC, Canada V6J 1Z1
www.namastepublishing.com

Distributed by PGW, Berkeley, CA USA

Cover design by Barbara Aronica

Interior book design by David Farr, ImageSmythe
                        Steve Amarillo, Urban Design LLC

Author photo by Bill "Butch r" Baker

Printed and bound in the United States by Malloy Incorporated,
Ann Arbor, MI

SUSTAINABLE FORESTRY INITIATIVE
Label applies to the text stock
Certified Fiber Sourcing
www.sfiprogram.org

Contents

1   The Experiment Begins   7

Imagine that your mind can transcend boundaries of space and time to join with every other mind that has ever or will ever read these words, enabling miracles to come more easily to us all.

2   What Did You Just Do?   11

That our minds reading the same words could form a very real, synergistic connection may seem farfetched, but the realization of a connection of consciousness may be just a short step away from becoming commonplace for us.

29 **A Return to Our Heart's Desires**   165

Let's return to our personal heart's desires, recognizing
there truly is no difference between one's own highest
good and that of others. As we act in service to our
personal well-being, we become more empowered to
serve the world. As we serve the world, we naturally
attract all we need to thrive.

30 **Taking a Quantum Leap**   171

If you're game—and here is where only the hardcore
believers need step forward—let's undertake an
experiment that's never been done. What can you
expect from it? Be open to no less than the fulfillment
of your dreams. Just don't expect anything expected.
Life may never be the same again!

Acknowledgments

BY THE TIME I GOT AROUND TO WRITING the acknowledgments for this book, I was so weary from the copy editing review that I just wanted to write, "I'm sick and tired of this book, thank you very much!" and leave it at that.

But I know the enlivening power of gratitude—I teach it, in fact. (I think spiritual teachers invariably wind up teaching what we need to learn so that we'll learn to practice what we preach!) So I pushed past my resistance and applied myself to the project with a hunch that it would take me somewhere I needed to go.

Without a thought in my head, I started to write. The words flowed and when it was done, I was surprised by what came out. The process clarified who and what have been most instrumental, not just in the writing of this book, but in the formation of my Self. When I finished, my weariness had been replaced with excitement, gratitude, and love, even for people I didn't always like so much along the way. I encourage everyone to write your own "Acknowledgments." Don't wait until you write a book!

—◆—

Thank you to everyone I've ever known who failed to live up to my expectations. Your participation in my life has helped me see my blocks, my flaws, and ultimately my strengths as I transform the illusion that my happiness is somehow determined by you. I thank you for playing this difficult role in my life. If you hadn't been there, I wouldn't know my Self the way I do.

I give thanks for the dark-night-of-the-soul years when I doubted my own teachings. Who knew—until it was over—that it was God's way of breaking down my walls of stubborn self-sufficiency so that I would accept a softer, gentler way of life?

I thank the unseen spiritual helpers who have guided the writing and publishing of this book in quite insistent (even bossy) ways. I couldn't have done it without you.

Thanks to Linda Hatfield and Cynthia Houtz, the wonderful people who have been working with me in recent years, enabling my work to grow bigger than one person can manage alone. And thanks to Laurie Dama and Alex Baker who have more recently joined the team. Thank you all for your support, great talents, and friendship.

Thanks to Michael Ulm for great collaboration and healing miracles!

Thanks to the folks at ImageSmythe who helped with the editing and design of the first, self-published release of this book and to Will Hale for passing the book, along to Constance Kellough of Namaste Publishing. A big thank you and "Namaste" to Constance for your enthusiastic support, as well as for your long-standing dedication to making the world a better place. Thanks as well to Managing Editor Lucinda Beacham for helping to make the second edition of this book, better than the first. Thanks to the whole Namaste team for being so delightful to work with.

A very special thanks goes to my husband Bill, who has unconditionally supported me through this project, loving me, believing in me, and even joining me in the work. With you, it's all fun!

Last, but far from least, I thank you, my readers. More than with any other writing project I've ever done, I felt your presence as I wrote and feel your presence with me still. Thank you for being willing to experiment with me.

Miracles

A miracle is
an event born in
unconditional love.

A miracle has a
healing ripple effect
on everyone it
touches.

A miracle is an occurrence that surpasses our
expectations and beliefs about what is possible.

Miracles include instantaneous manifestations,
marvelous coincidences, and impossible healings.

Miracles are God in action.

Miracles are faith made tangible.

Miracles reshape our definition of reality.

Miracles dissipate fear, despair, hatred, and pain.

Miracles help us to know our Oneness with all life.

Miracles show us that we are never separate from God.

Miracles teach us that Love is the only true power there is.

Miracles lead to uncontrolled outbreaks of inner peace and joy.

Miracles arise from uncontrolled outbreaks of inner peace and joy.

Miracles demonstrate the awesome power we have to
change our lives
and to change the
world around us.

Introduction

THE PERFECT PARKING PLACE SHOWS UP EVERY TIME. A hopelessly lost pet reappears within an hour of a group praying for a miracle. The perfect house becomes available, a job opens, money multiplies, the right people appear, all through serendipity too remarkable to be "coincidence."

I don't *believe* in miracles like these; I see them in my daily life. I would no more say I believe in miracles than say I believe in cars, or planes, or chairs. They're just a part of life.

For decades, a rash of literature has shown how easy it is to create miraculous health, wealth, and happiness by following the simplest of formulas or techniques. Many wonderful books have taught us the value of affirmations and visualization, of practicing meditation and yoga, of positive thinking and prayer. Popular movies like *What the Bleep Do We Know?!* and *The Secret* make "the Law of Attraction" look like an easy way to have everything we want. And it really is that easy—except, of course, when it's not, when no amount of affirmation or visualization techniques will budge life circumstances that feel hopelessly out of our control. Sometimes these techniques backfire comically with results that are literally just what we asked for, as when a woman I once knew affirmed, "My next boyfriend is rich!" Her affirmation produced immediate results, drawing into her life a new boyfriend who wasn't wealthy but was named Rich!

While I will address the art of intentional manifestation and spontaneous healing here, miracle-making goes beyond either of these. Too often the practices of spiritual healing or intentional manifestation keep our focus on the presence of disease or on a lack of something in our lives. Miracles may include healings and manifestations, but they take us beyond our needs, beyond our wants, and beyond the limitations of our thinking. They're such a direct experience of God energy that they don't simply produce a desired outcome; they change us.

For example, several days after attending one of my group experiments, a woman came into a large windfall of money after her sister won the lottery and shared it with her. The money definitely helped the woman progress speedily toward the goals she had identified at the group event. But when she recounted the story, she said the real miracle wasn't the manifested money; it was that her sister shared it with her. The two had had a very strained relationship and this gesture produced a totally unexpected healing. Miracles can result in all kinds of lovely manifestations, but they're more than these end products. Miracles are always rooted in love, the love of God that transforms us and makes all things possible.

Calling forth a miracle is a bit like coaxing some beautiful, wild thing out of the woods. When you find you can't chase it down or catch it, you finally give up hunting and just become still. Yet merely stopping the chase isn't enough; the thing won't come out as long as it senses your agitation. You need to relax. Then you look the other way, because the creature is shy and won't appear if it knows you're waiting for it. So you pretend to be simply enjoying the day with no other agenda. After a while, you actually are enjoying yourself, peaceful and content, the wild thing all but forgotten—when suddenly there it is, magical and magnificent, better than you expected, coming right to you.

And it comes just as you've stopped trying, stopped expending effort, aren't even focused on it anymore, so its appearance feels strangely not in your control. Certainly you did things. You wanted it, you set an intention for it, you looked, and you waited. But these things by themselves didn't call the creature forth. It was the point of release, a simple lightness of being and love of life that called the wild miracle.

Stop for a minute before reading on. Think about whether you experienced anything as you read this last paragraph. Did you put yourself in the words and picture something wild and beautiful out there watching you as you waited for it? And did you, just for a moment, release the feeling of "hunting" as you imagined the easier experience of simply being present and light? If you did, you've already altered your vibration a bit to let something wonderful sneak into your life when you least expect it.

This book won't give you a never-fail formula for manifesting miracles—because there isn't one. It will explain some of the science and psychology of miracles, which is important, because many of us will block what we don't understand. It will also offer stories of real life miracles, because the more commonplace they seem, the easier it is to relax, to stop stalking the impossible miracles, and to let them simply appear on their own terms. Most important of all, I'll walk you through some experiments and playful moments in which, together, we can forget what's impossible long enough to let the miraculous slip through!

You don't need to read this book in a straight line from beginning to end in order to see miraculous manifestations. Miracles aren't linear. You might experience the most phenomenal miracle of your life after reading the very next page or by opening the book anywhere. What reading this book from start to finish will do is help you to accept and truly benefit from miracles. Each chapter contains an exercise and/or an experiment in miracle-making. The exercises prepare you for the experiments, and the experiments take you beyond time and space into uncharted territory to see what is possible. If you give careful attention to each one, you're likely to notice fortunate coincidences and serendipities happening more frequently. You also may experience dramatic life changes.

Alternately, change may creep up on you so slowly that you don't notice it at all until one day you realize everything is different. This was the case with a woman who attended a healing event with me. She reported many months later that she didn't realize she had been healed of a severe, chronic, asthma condition until she found herself in a situation that would normally trigger an attack. As she noticed she was fine, it dawned on her she couldn't remember the last time she'd had an attack, because it had been so long.

As with the wild thing in the woods, don't stalk your miracles. Give yourself over to the quality of the moment, and let your miracles find you—in great, obvious ways or in quiet, secret ones.

I suggest doing the experiments when you have some quiet time to yourself. Some of them are a bit long. For best results, you can either read them slowly in a quiet, reflective state, make a recording to listen to with your eyes closed, or use my recordings that are available on CD or for download at www. namastepublishing.com

Perhaps the best way of all to experience this book is with a study group, where you can discuss the exercises and do the experiments together, reading them aloud as guided meditations. The butterflies appear in the text to help you pause between thoughts so when you see them, breathe, reflect, be still. 🦋 🦋 🦋

Every segment of the book builds upon the next, from this introduction on, with the aim of helping us all—readers and author alike—to grow, not just a miraculous result or two, but a thoroughly miraculous life. Probably the most effective way to go through this book is to work with the material of each chapter, giving at least a day to each exercise before going on to the next chapter. However you choose to plunge into this experiment, I hope you enjoy the ride!

1
The Experiment Begins

THIS BOOK IS AN INVITATION TO SUSPEND DISBELIEF, let your mind be boggled, and have an experience of reality beyond what you think you know for certain. Miracles are more readily found in the slightly unsettling territory of paradox than on familiar ground so, if you're game, let the experiment begin right now by imagining that the earth is shifting just a bit underfoot and that nothing you see is what it appears to be.

The more of this book you read, the more deeply you will enter into a miracle-making experiment. Modern science, as you will learn, is showing we can't change our minds without affecting the world around us and, as easily as reading these pages, your mind and your world are changing. If it's your choice, you will become a miracle-maker. And if you're feeling excited, it's already begun.

Proceed a little further into the experiment by imagining you're not alone as you read. Change your mind about the normally solitary experience of reading so that you are now, simply through your intention to do so, linking with every other mind who is reading these words. As we'll explore in greater depth, all consciousness is connected. To quote one of the pioneers of modern physics, Erwin Schrödinger, on the nature of consciousness, "The overall number of minds is just one."

To wade a little more deeply into the fuzzy edges of reality, let go of what you think you know about time. Einstein proved in his theory of relativity that time and space aren't a fixed, neutral container for matter and can be altered by what they contain. Time is a more fluid thing than we realize, as Helmut Schmidt, one of the early researchers of mind over matter, discovered in his extensive work with random event generators. He not only found statistically significant evidence suggesting consciousness alone can indeed affect matter, but also that consciousness can affect matter *in the past*. More on this later.

For now, without quite understanding how, imagine your mind is transcending the fluid boundaries of time and space to connect with every mind that has in the past, and will in the future, read these words. This is happening automatically, simply because you're thinking it. You don't even need to believe it; just imagine what it would feel like if you did.

Picture this joined consciousness as clear, beautiful, and only positive. As we join minds, we leave behind the clutter of small, weak thoughts that so often cloud our attention, and we rise into a Higher Mind that is wise and wonderful. In this Higher Mind, we amplify each other's power for good and automatically repel harm. You may already feel a difference. Your senses may be a little sharper; you might feel warmth or tingling or gooseflesh. Perhaps you're a little more awake. You may notice your body is relaxing and you're breathing more deeply. You may feel nothing at all, the real magic happening outside of your conscious awareness. It doesn't matter what you perceive. Just imagine what it would be like if you felt certain, beyond a shadow of a doubt, that miracles are normal and starting to unfold in your life.

Now, for a moment, hold the deepest, most heartfelt intention that every reader of these words, past, present, and future, receive something wonderful, and imagine just by reading this page, you will too. Hold this thought lightly and with wonder, like you would a butterfly that just alit in your hand. 🦋 Hold it gently, no need to strain, and now let it go. Just as anonymous prayer has been shown to have a definite healing effect, even when the recipients are unaware that prayer is being offered on their behalf, just this easily, a powerful prayer has now been set in motion on your behalf.

After this exercise, if you notice a waft of rose scent that has no discernible source or you see butterflies, feathers, or some cherished symbol wherever you go, just say thank you. As you've opened yourself to God, God is showing Itself to you.

And now you've become more than a passive reader—you've become part of this experiment, reshaping matter and calling forth miracles for yourself and countless others whom you will never know.

2

What Did You Just Do?

THE CONCEPT OF COLLECTIVE CONSCIOUSNESS is both modern and ancient. Metaphysicians call this collective mind the "Akashik Record" and see it as a universal container of all information. Carl Jung, an early father of psychology, called it the "collective unconscious" and helped people access it through dreams. A Nobel Prize–winning physicist of the early twentieth century, Erwin Schrödinger, spoke of there being "one mind," theorizing that our individual minds contributed to one universal mind.

Research into consciousness is suggesting the way information on the World Wide Web comes through our home computer (rather than from it) may be a precise model for how our brains access information. Mounting evidence from the edges of quantum science is showing the presence of an energy field, the Zero Point Field—essentially a quantum soup of energy underpinning all existence—and that this field, not the brain, is the true repository of memory and information. The brain acts more like an individual computer accessing information from a collective, external pool.*

---

*Hal Puthoff and Walter Schempp have been two groundbreakers in bringing this idea of zero point energy to light.

Author Donald Dulchinos, a veteran of the cable TV industry and involved in online communities predating the World Wide Web, pulled together many fascinating strands of philosophy, technology, and science in his book *Neurosphere* on "the convergence of evolution, group mind, and the Internet." He presents the views of numbers of well-known theorists, many predating the Internet, who all believe humanity is moving in the direction of a higher, wiser, group mind. The chaos theorist, Ralph Abraham, for example, believes the explosive growth of the World Wide Web has actually increased the bandwidth of the mind's connections and increased the overall intelligence of our species. The early twentieth-century philosopher Pierre Teilhard de Chardin anticipated this quickening of human consciousness in his theory that as humans stopped evolving biologically, they began an evolution of consciousness. Dulchinos writes, "The World Wide Web is the material manifestation of Teilhard's vision." He himself speculates that "the Internet represents the latest manifestation, in the material world, of the ongoing evolution of consciousness."

This book, and what you just did when you imagined your mind linking with those of others reading this book, are simply a next step in this evolution of human consciousness. Many threads of research, a small few of which we'll touch on in these pages, are demonstrating the amazing power a single mind has to affect the physical world, the exponentially greater power of many minds joined in a common intention, and the unbounded power of minds to transcend not just spatial limitations but even time. What you just did in the preceding exercise was to join the very real energy of your consciousness with that of all the minds who have read and *will read* these words. This repeated joining of many minds across time and space creates an energy field that becomes a force in its own right.

The modern-day biochemist Rupert Sheldrake coined the term "morphic field" to describe this field, relating it to the cumulative memory of species as well as human systems of thought. These morphic fields exist beyond time and space, are developed through repetition, and make it easier and easier, like a worn pathway, for subsequent individuals to follow in the same pattern.

Through intention and repetition we create and tap a synergistic force exponentially greater than ourselves. In this way, it becomes easier for each of us to experience results in alignment with our common intention than we ever could alone. You could think of what we're doing as being a little like many computers joined on a network so that each has the resources of every computer on the network—except that with consciousness the amplifying effect is exponential rather than merely the sum of all the parts.

We'll look at this idea in greater depth later, but for now, to put it very simplistically: alone, we work as separate particles and, consequently, are slowed by the natural laws of the physical world. This physical world requires a linear series of steps to get from point A to point B, and movement can only happen through time and physical intervention. Together, however, our thoughts, our actions, even our very physicality become wave-like and work through the very different laws of quantum reality. In this quantum reality, points A and B are integrally connected parts of a unified energy soup, and movement between any two points can happen instantaneously—like electricity traveling through water—with no steps, time, or physical intervention required. In this world, movement is fueled by consciousness.

That minds reading the same words could form a very real and synergistic connection may seem farfetched right now but, just as the incredible connectivity and resources that the Internet provides were undreamed of short decades ago, the connection of consciousness described here may, too, be just a short step away from becoming commonplace.

Exercise
Bright Point of Light in an Energy Sea

For our first exercise, imagine yourself as a very bright point of light in an energy sea. Imagine there are many, many points of light in this sea, in the same way there are countless drops of water in the ocean. In this energy sea, time is nonexistent. The past, present, and future all exist at once. Picture the other people reading these words (past, present, and future) as being other points of light in this sea. You don't need to believe any of this. Just think it and see whether you can make it come to life in your imagination.

Simply by intending it, you can now see energy currents connecting you to all of these other readers. These connections were there before, because everything in this sea is connected, but now you light them up; you cause them to vibrate together. You can't see how many are connected in this network of light, but you can sense a powerful energy field now present and growing stronger. This energy field is purely a force for good and brings out the best in everyone touched by it. Those in the network feel it most intensely and ripple it outward so, ultimately, the vibration is felt throughout the whole sea.

Spend a day imagining yourself now part of a vibrating network of transformative energy that's gently lifting you into a wave of peace. This wave is comforting and easy. It helps you rise easily to meet the challenges of life and clears away whatever obstacles aren't necessary. Joining this wave is as easy as floating downstream on a quiet river, so don't work at it—just enjoy it.

3

Miracles Are Natural

"Miracles are natural. When they do not occur, something has gone wrong."

—A COURSE IN MIRACLES

A miracle, as I'm defining it here, is an event born in unconditional love. It has a healing ripple effect on everyone it touches, and seems to defy the laws of the natural world, as wonderful results unfold by way of serendipity rather than effort. It has a win-win, positive outcome that shows up in an instantaneous, coincidental way. Such an event often feels beyond what we thought could happen, so our beliefs about what's possible stretch a little wider.

Although I have been deeply involved in the study and teaching of metaphysics, spiritual healing, and transpersonal psychology since the early 1970s, it wasn't until I encountered the work of Dr. Gerald Jampolsky that the word *miracle* truly entered my vocabulary. The psychiatrist and best-selling author of *Love is Letting Go of Fear* made a big splash in the 1980s by going on national television with children from his Center for Attitudinal Healing in Tiburon, California. The children told stories of their seemingly incurable diseases healing as they simply practiced principles of attitudinal healing": letting go of fear, living in the moment, and extending unconditional love. Dr. Jampolsky drew the philosophy of attitudinal healing from *A Course in Miracles*, a lengthy three-volume text of spiritual philosophy and lessons that guide students through a step-by-step process of shifting perception from fear to love. The Center for Attitudinal Healing, which still offers free support services for children and adults dealing with health crises, inspired the formation of similar centers around the world and inspired me as well to help found and direct the Baltimore Center for Attitudinal Healing in 1983.

At our center, we saw the same kind of healing miracles Jerry's kids experienced, and sick children who weren't supposed to get better did. What's more, as I worked more deeply with the fundamental principles underlying the philosophy of attitudinal healing and taught them to our staff of volunteers, we found that miracles started happening for all of us, often in everyday matters, not just life-and-death issues. Understanding how and why miracles happen became my passion, so in 1987 I left the Baltimore Center for Attitudinal Healing to extend my teaching of miracle principles beyond the context of illness and crisis.

After decades of this work, I've seen so many people experience synchronicities and dramatic, fortunate "coincidences" occurring in tandem with open-hearted states of joy and awakening that I no longer see anything coincidental about it. And, along with a myriad of beautiful serendipities, I've also witnessed phenomena that are so dramatic they can't even pose as coincidence—miracles of the mind-boggling, how-can-that-possibly-be? variety. Over the years I've had the opportunity to work with and observe a number of gifted healers whose practice includes not just the spontaneous disappearance of all sorts of physical ailments but, in some cases, the very rare phenomenon of dental fillings spontaneously turning to gold, silver, or porcelain right before our eyes. If this last one seems completely out of your comfort zone to even consider, I urge you to read on. I'll explain more about this phenomenon in later chapters, as well as some of my first-hand experiences with one particularly gifted practitioner.

I have found the work of these healing miracle-makers to be important, not just for the suffering they relieve, but because they demonstrate the incredible range of what's possible. The down side I've noticed is one can easily become reliant on the healer when such a powerful result comes through a single individual. Instead of miracles feeling naturally accessible to all, as in attitudinal healing groups where everyone is equal, they seem to be the healer's alone to dispense.

If you consider yourself capable of "small" miracles but draw a line in your mind at a certain point, recognize that there is no magnitude of difficulty to miracles. The only limitation is your own thinking. Even if you don't believe yourself to have the abilities of a gifted miracle-maker, we have an added ingredient to draw upon here: all of us together. We are doing something together that's never been done, and before we're through, I believe you will realize that there are no miracles too big for God to work through you. All that needs changing is your mind and, as our journey continues, this will happen more easily than you might think.

What does it mean when miracles become "natural," as *A Course in Miracles* claims them to be? Perhaps it means that we seek and trust God's intervention in our lives first, instead of when all other resources have been exhausted. A woman in my weekly class, who was a bit of a skeptic, at my suggestion simply started a practice of asking God's help in finding parking places where they tended to be scarce. She did it playfully without a lot of expectations. To her amazement, it worked every time with a convenient place becoming available just as she needed it. She went on to have more and more experiences of helpful serendipity.

Another story of miracles flowing naturally comes from a young man who was in one of my workshops many years ago. He told us how he decided to move to a big city, showing up homeless, jobless, penniless, and friendless. He kept saying to himself, not as an affirmation technique but because he truly meant it, "I don't know what's going to happen, but I know it's going to be great!" And he really did feel himself to be on a wonderful adventure. With astonishing speed and serendipity, one thing after another fell into place for him—a place to stay, a job, friends—and soon his new life was well underway. This is miracle-consciousness in action. Excitement, anticipation, wonder, and trusting in the process of life all create the fertile ground for miracles to spring up. So today simply allow yourself to become excited about miracles.

Exercise
Anything can happen, and it's going to be great!

Spend today living like this young man. Imagine yourself setting out on a great adventure. Reality, as you've known it, has been suspended and you've entered a window where miracles can happen, where anything is possible. On the outside, your life may look as humdrum as ever, but inside, every fiber of your being recognizes that miracles are in the air and knows something wonderful is about to happen. You don't know what, but you know it's going to be great! You don't even need to fully believe this. Simply imagine what it would feel like if you did. As you go about your day, see whether you can feel the very air charged with this sense of something wonderful about to happen. Remind yourself often that you don't know what's going to happen, but you know it's going to be great! Let your feelings of excitement, wonder, and anticipation build all day.

4

Impossible Miracles

ONCE A WOMAN ALMOST DIDN'T ATTEND a three-day workshop I led on healing, because she was so emotionally distraught over the loss of her beloved cat just weeks before. The cat had escaped the house and not been recovered in spite of enormous efforts by many people to search and poster the area. She was deeply grieving the loss of her "best friend" and wasn't sure she was fit to be around people, but she finally decided a three-day healing retreat would do her good.

In the first hour of the workshop I talked briefly about miracles, then asked people to identify a miracle they really wanted for themselves that felt too impossibly big to believe it could happen over the course of the weekend. This woman identified the return of her cat as being her most longed-for and impossible miracle; the second most impossible was the healing of the severe physical pain and disability she'd had ever since a car accident many years earlier. Shortly thereafter, her cell phone rang, disturbing our session, and she hurriedly turned it off. Upon checking her messages at the break, she found the "interruption" was a call from someone who had found her cat, skinny but safe. Her miracles didn't stop there. On the second day of the workshop, she arrived not needing the canes she had been using for years, and she did a little dance for us to prove it! All this happened before we had even begun the hands-on healing work of the weekend.

Miracles don't require time, effort, exercises, or even "positive thinking," and no amount of study, training, or practice can guarantee one. Yet, they can be as simple and accessible as a daydream.

Exercise
What's Too Impossible?

Spend today reflecting on all the miracles your heart longs for but you're sure are too big to happen. Let yourself daydream about them, even if—especially if—you think they're impossible.

5

The Science of Miracles

HE RELATIVELY NEW SCIENCE OF CONSCIOUSNESS is now explaining the mechanics of the miraculous in ways even the most skeptical thinkers are beginning to embrace. Melvin Morse, M.D., best-selling author of *Closer to the Light* and well-known researcher of near-death experiences, goes so far as to suggest that the current debate between "skeptics" and "believers" has become obsolete because it's based upon old science.*

So we no longer have to "believe." We just need to be paying attention to know that consciousness is powerful, joined beyond time and space, and capable of far more than we know. The findings of quantum physics for more than a century now have introduced many mind-boggling paradoxes that are completely changing our previous understanding of matter, time, space, and consciousness, proving beyond a shadow of a doubt that the physical world cannot be neatly observed, measured, and predicted as once thought. Physics is proving what spiritual traditions have taught for years: a reality exists beyond what we can see and know through the limited perceptions of our physical senses.

---

*For an interesting and fairly quick read, check out Morse's book, *Where God Lives*, which explores through anecdotes and science the existence of a universal energy pattern outside the body, where memory is stored—much like a World Wide Web of consciousness.

To explain briefly, for more than a couple of centuries now the Newtonian model of reality has prevailed. This view holds that the universe, be it at the macrocosmic level of planets or the microcosmic level of atoms, is mechanical. It is made of separate components that move and interact in predictable ways that can be observed, precisely measured, and expected to behave the same way at every observation.

But during the last century, scientists have shown the seemingly solid, predictable nature of matter to be more complex and miraculous than we had ever imagined. We now know matter does not behave consistently at the subatomic level. Instead, it shows statistical *tendencies* to behave in certain patterns *and* has the potential to change spontaneously in ways that have no clearly apparent physical cause. What's more, at this quantum level, matter can exhibit the qualities of solid, separate particles *and* the qualities of unified light waves. The way matter shows up has to do with the way it is observed. In other words, when the scientist-observer is looking for particles, particles are found and have characteristics exclusive to particles. But when the observer is looking for waves, waves are found and have characteristics exclusive to waves. As physicist Fred Alan Wolf writes about this phenomenon in *Taking the Quantum Leap,* "How matter appears depends on our minds' choices; reality is a 'matter' of choice."

Another of the many mind-bending findings of quantum physics shows that at the quantum level motion doesn't happen in the linear, flowing, "point A to point B" way we had assumed. Instead, subatomic particles have been observed to "leap" from one place to another, all at once, without passing through the space in between—something impossible to explain using the old Newtonian model of reality.

We can no longer even trust time and space to be the known quantities we perceive with our physical senses. In the words of well-known physicist Stephen Hawking, "[Einstein's] theory of relativity combined time with space and said that both could be warped or distorted by the matter and energy in the universe...."

No longer could we think of space and time as running on forever, unaffected by what happened in the universe.... Instead, they were now dynamic quantities that influenced and were influenced by events that took place in them."

Along these lines, Helmut Schmidt of the Mind Science Foundation in San Antonio, Texas, conducted extensive research on the power of consciousness to affect matter, using random event generators that produced random patterns such as those produced by radioactive decay. His studies, which have been successfully replicated by other researchers, showed undeniable evidence that mental intention could influence these random patterns, proving thought alone can influence matter. But that's not all. His experiments showed that subjects could not only mentally influence random patterns occurring in the present; they could also affect random results that had been collected in the past. More recent research on time, some of which we'll touch upon in future chapters, is suggesting even more fantastic possibilities for all the ways we can change the past with conscious intention.

It's becoming increasingly clear the universe isn't simply an assembly of separate particles, planets, and entities in set, predictable relationships to one another. Instead, we're finding all the pieces making up our physical world are dynamic, interrelated, and able to affect and be affected by one another. It's impossible, even, to separate ourselves from the whole sufficiently to observe it without our very observations having an impact.

These new truths, by their very nature, must radically reshape how we perceive ourselves and our relationships to one another, and how we live day to day and relate to the world around us. Taken out of the realm of science and applied to daily life, these new laws of physics suggest a reality in which we have far more power to influence our environment than we've previously known. Our very thoughts have the power to affect the physical world, and movement at the physical level can happen instantaneously, through a "leap" in time and space rather than

r, mechanical process. The only limitations are the ones
impose on ourselves with our fixed beliefs and assumptions
about life.

Exercise
Let Go of What You Think You Know

Imagine that all you thought you knew for certain is not true.
Don't assume this means the opposite is true or what you
most fear is true. You don't need to figure out what *is* true or
to understand the how and why of this. Simply play with it
as an exercise in imagination. As you release your current
interpretations, don't immediately grasp for new ones. Simply
let your mind open, and allow yourself to be confused. This
process is much like letting your eyes go out of focus so you're
seeing the color, form, and the big picture of the world around
you rather than the details. Imagine that, even in the midst of
confusion and not knowing, you're safe and at peace.

Begin by looking down at the ground beneath your feet and
saying to yourself, "Nothing I think I know for certain about
the ground beneath my feet is true." Then look up and say to
yourself, "Nothing I think I know for certain about the room
around me is true" or "Nothing I think I know for certain about
the sky above my head is true." Then look around at objects and
do the same. Next, do the same with people, your relationships,
circumstances, theories, and most importantly, yourself. Play
with this exercise all day and apply it to everything.

6

We Create Our Reality

T HE NOTION THAT OUR VERY THOUGHT affects the physical world around us is a heady concept that tends to give rise to more questions than answers. If we can change our mind, does that mean we never need to be victims of circumstances beyond our control? Easy to say, but how does this work in practice?

Here's one of my own earliest experiences, decades ago, of what it means to create my own reality. I was still in my twenties at the time, and the idea that my outer life circumstances could be directly reflecting my inner state was a brand-new concept to me. I understood it in theory, but it hadn't fully sunk in yet. On this particular day, I had a million things to do. Paperwork (all with imminent deadlines) piled up at my office. I had a class to teach that evening and hadn't even started preparing for it. But instead of attending to all this, I was at a busy shopping mall about to pay an overdue phone bill my housemates were supposed to have taken care of before leaving on a month-long vacation. In this era before cell phones and online bill paying, my only phone was scheduled to be disconnected the next day if I didn't immediately hand deliver enough money to cover my housemates' large long-distance bills. I was stressed over money, furious at my housemates, and suffering a splitting headache.

As I walked impatiently through the mall searching for the phone company office, I accidentally kicked myself in the ankle so hard that it stopped me in my tracks and sent blood trickling into my shoe. When I could move again, I limped the remaining distance to my destination only to discover the longest line I'd ever seen. I almost broke down in tears when I realized the long wait I had ahead of me.

With nothing to do but stand there, I was left alone with my thoughts. I thought of how I had kicked myself and wondered if it was just the most obvious example of how I'd been "kicking" myself all day in many different ways. This strange new concept that my thoughts create my reality popped into mind, and I shuddered to think of what this day's batch of thoughts must be creating. Since I had nothing else to do, I thought I'd see if I could change my thoughts right then and there as I stood in the phone company bill-paying line.

I was so distressed, I knew concentrating on "happy thoughts" and positive affirmations wouldn't do the job, so instead I started by simply forgiving myself. I forgave myself for being angry, for feeling unsupported, for not meeting my own expectations of perfection, for "kicking myself." As I reflected, it occurred to me that in my overwhelmed state I didn't feel "grownup" at all; I felt about four years old. I pursued this thought further and pictured myself as I felt: small, fearful, more abandoned than angry. And then, instead of feeling angry at myself, I began to feel compassion.

The knot in my stomach relaxed, my mind stopped racing, and my heart softened. Deep in my own thoughts at this point, I had long since stopped noticing the slow-moving line. Instead, I imagined taking my own small self in my arms and comforting her, letting her rage until her anger turned to fear and sadness. I realized that underlying the angry urge to kick someone (myself, as it turned out) was the vulnerability of feeling alone with the burdens of life and a desire to be taken care of. In my imagination, I gave that care to myself.

As the image faded away, I suddenly realized I was at the beginning of the payment line. I paid my bill and left, a different person than I had been twenty minutes earlier. In spite of my head still hurting, I was at peace, not worrying about my class or money or anything anymore.

And the Miracles Began

When I returned to my office, I found a message that had come in while I was at the mall. It was from a woman in the class I was to teach that evening, who said she had a special presentation she wanted to make to the group that evening if I would be willing to put off whatever I had planned. As I had nothing planned, this couldn't have been a more welcomed request. Minutes later, I opened my mail and found a substantial check made out to me with a note that the giver had been so inspired by my work she wanted to make a tithe to me. It covered the phone bill with some left over.

The rest of the afternoon flowed by easily and I breezed through the work I needed to complete. I arrived at my class several hours later. Almost as soon as I walked in the door, a class member who was a skilled healing practitioner took one look at me and saw that I needed some healing attention. While the woman with the special presentation led my class, the healing practitioner relieved my headache with Reiki healing and massage, and I thoroughly enjoyed letting other people take care of me for the rest of the evening.

On this day I truly "got it." I understood the connection between my thoughts and my life. And what was most striking to me was how little effort it took to transform this horrible day into one of the nicest I had had in a long time.

Making this shift doesn't need to be hard work. It's simply a choice to focus attention differently. Perhaps the hardest part is catching ourselves in the midst of a downward spiral and recognizing that we do, in fact, have a choice.

y hour or so, just stop and notice your frame of mind. If it's ს .ne form of happiness, peace, contentedness, gratefulness, or lovingness, enjoy it, and consciously amplify it. If there's stress, consider doing this exercise, which I think of as "emergency care" to stop a bad day midstream and turn it around.

STEP ONE

Stop. Stop whatever you're doing that isn't bringing you peace. Stop talking, stop worrying, stop trying to figure things out, stop running from one thing to another, and stop proving you're right or trying to be perfect. Stop controlling.

STEP TWO

Close your eyes (or, if you happen to be in the middle of a shopping mall, simply turn your attention inward) and take a few deep breaths. Relax. Let your shoulders drop. Let the muscles in your stomach relax. Feel your brow become smooth and free of worry lines.

STEP THREE

Take a moment to simply be with whatever you're feeling without judging it or trying to change it. If it's rage, sadness, or despair, just let it be there. If there's fear, guilt, or self-pity, just be aware of it. Notice how it sits in your body rather than noticing what you think about it.

STEP FOUR

Ask yourself, how old do I feel right now? Don't think too hard about this. Simply let an age pop into your mind or an image of a younger you appear in your mind's eye.

STEP FIVE

Ask yourself, "As me at this age, what do I need now?" Don't concern yourself with what you needed then. Rather than going into old family history, imagine what the childlike feelings in you now are calling out for. For example, as I stood in the phone line, if I asked my adult self that question, she would have answered, "I need my housemates to be more responsible! I need more money! I need to get back to my office and get some work done!" However, the four-year-old feeling had an entirely different answer. First she wanted to kick and scream and rage. The tantrum quickly gave way to wanting to be taken care of, wanting to be held, wanting to have somebody notice her pain. She wanted things that my adult self wouldn't have admitted to.

STEP SIX

Use your imagination to create an inner experience in which your child self gets whatever it needs. You might imagine an angelic protector holding you while you cry, keeping you safe while you have a tantrum, or taking you on a magic carpet ride where you can feel free and rise above stress. You might imagine yourself as an adult caring for your child self. Play with different images and scenarios until you find one that gives a sense of release, relief, and comfort. As your imagery becomes vivid, you are actually changing the vibration you emit to the world that draws stressful circumstances into your life. Think of it this way: as you inwardly treat yourself kindly, you teach the world to treat you gently, as well.

STEP SEVEN

Let this imagery experience go when it reaches a natural completion and you find a feeling of relief. As you go back to the activities of your day, consciously choose to interrupt any thoughts that want to plunge you back into the day you were having.

As you do this exercise, let your only goal be to feel peaceful in the here and now. Don't do it with expectations of dazzling results, because this train of thought will distract you from simply being present. The value of this exercise is in finding acceptance and joy in the face of what is, so instead of expecting results, just enjoy the moment.

7
Our Power Together

CONSCIOUSNESS IS A POWERFUL FORCE, and when we join in a common intent with other minds, an amplifying effect occurs that is far greater than the sum of the individuals. Things that were difficult to achieve separately suddenly become easy when we join together. Anyone who has ever found it easier to meditate with a group than alone has experienced this phenomenon.

But there are other, more dramatic applications of this as well. For example, if you put your hand in the lit coals of your backyard barbecue grill, do you believe it would burn? Of course you do, and it most likely would. Yet if you were to attend a guided fire-walking event and spend an evening with a group of people joining together in faith that the fire wouldn't hurt, it probably wouldn't. Many ordinary people have attended such events and successfully walked on impossibly hot coals with little or no blistering.

Through the rigorous discipline of a life devoted to meditation, Tibetan Buddhist monks are known to be able to regulate their bodies in seemingly impossible ways to adapt to extreme temperatures. In 1985, Harvard Medical School cardiologist Herbert Benson witnessed monks in India sit nearly naked in near-freezing conditions, being draped continuously with ice cold, wet sheets. Instead of freezing to death, their bodies radiated so much heat that steam rose from the sheets, drying them within an hour. This level of control takes years to accomplish, yet groups of inexperienced firewalkers achieve successful mastery over their element in just hours.

Spoon-bending workshops in which people are taught in a very short amount of time to make metal utensils behave like Silly Putty are a similar kind of group event that has become popular in recent years. Workshops like these teach us to bend, not just spoons, but the very rules of reality as we know them, and do it astonishingly quickly.

Both fire-walking and spoon-bending events start with at least one person who has a solid faith in the process based, not in hopefulness, but in the certainty of having seen it work before. Faith is highly contagious. One person with particularly powerful faith can spark the faith of a whole group. Then the amplifying power of group consciousness kicks in, setting in motion a wavelike energy that lifts everyone, even those still in doubt. The combination of group intention and the guidance of at least one person with unshakable faith can quickly lift a whole group of people to possibilities that would be difficult to manifest individually.

I've seen this dynamic produce powerful results countless times in my own group experiments. Personally, I like to come away with something more interesting than a bent spoon or blister-free feet, so for the following experiment, we will set the intention for something miraculous to happen in the coming week.

Experiment
Say "YES!" to Miracles

As we enter into this experiment, I have the confident faith of someone who's seen countless miracles happen for many people in many groups, and I can lend my faith to you. I have so much confidence we'll create miracles together that it's not even necessary for you to have absolute faith yourself. / ... that's needed is your willingness and an open mind. (What was it Jesus said? It only takes a mustard seed's worth of faith to move a mountain. You don't need to be a Christian to recognize how much he knew about spiritual law.) We also have the amplifying power of many minds in all of you, past, present, and future, who are reading these words.

So don't worry about dispelling all doubt. Instead, simply give attention to your mustard seed of faith. Your imagination can help you with this: imagine how it would feel if you did have total faith. You might even imagine what it would feel like to be someone you know, or know of, whose faith is greater than yours. As you step out of yourself in this way and see through new eyes, you will experience a bigger faith. Even a moment of faith is a powerful force.

Relax into the present moment now, and imagine how it would feel to be absolutely certain something wonderful is about to happen; you don't know what but you know it's going to be great. Let excitement build palpably in your body. 🦋 🦋 🦋

Already we've started a wave of faith, and now we'll add the amplifying power of many minds together. Take a couple of deep breaths and relax a little more. 🦋 🦋 🦋 Let your mind become quiet and still, very focused on these words. Let the solid, predictable nature of reality as you have always known it soften a bit, allowing you to form an invisible link, outside of time and space, to many minds who, just like you, are reading these words. Picture the joined consciousness of us all as something clear and bright and purely benevolent. Though you may never know these others in a personal way, let them start to feel like friends. Picture this network in whatever way feels most supportive, vivid, and powerful.

Imagine us all joining in the common intention that many of us reading these words, even all of us, are going to experience miracles of all sorts: miraculous moments of "being," spontaneous healings, delightful synchronicities, new opportunities appearing, gifts and blessings of all sorts showing up unexpectedly, revelations, new directions opening, and more. You may find it easier to have faith in others' successes than your own, but that's okay. You don't have to have perfect faith in yourself because there are now many others who have great faith in you. Just as your faith flows more freely to them than to yourself, they're doing the same for you. Let go of wondering whether it's going to work, and imagine you've now jumped into a river of group consciousness that is lifting you effortlessly into potential you've never been able to tap before. Things that have been difficult will come more easily; things that were impossible for you alone are now within reach. Your highest good has begun to unfold beyond your wildest dreams.

Now give your permission for reality to operate differently than it ever has before. Give permission for miracles to become natural and easy. Say, "YES!" to miracles.

As you think of it during the day, keep saying "YES!" to miracles. Say it with joy rather than dogged determination. Keep it light. Repeat the word over and over to yourself, silently or out loud, and notice how it changes your state of mind and how your body feels. This is the feeling of your subconscious mind moving resistance out of the way so that miracles can happen.

It's like an ancient drawbridge that's huge, heavy, and looks impenetrable (like your unconscious doubts, resistance, and disbelief) until it opens for a fleet of tall ships (miracles coming your way). Your conscious mind is the tiny operator and your "YES!" turns on the opening mechanism, but it's your subconscious mind that does the heavy lifting. So, even if saying "YES!" seems a small and inconsequential gesture, know it is all that's needed to set an invisible process in motion.

As you fall asleep tonight, imagine a host of helpful beings made of light, representing the Higher Selves of other readers, who have joined together to support your highest good and well-being. Take comfort in their presence. Imagine this to be a benevolent force now operating on your behalf.

8

The Science of Light, Love, and God

IGHT: SO PURE AND PRIMAL it's perhaps one of our most-used metaphors. It stands for clarity, goodness, spirituality, and salvation from all things dark and frightening. Light is life-giving and divine. From the world of science, we know light, energy, and matter are all variations of the same. As quantum science demonstrates that most of reality goes on at a level imperceptible to our human senses, it's also showing the very underpinnings of the universe to consist of a field of light.

In the seventies, the highly distinguished physicist Hal Puthoff pioneered study into the mysteries of this energy field, called the Zero Point Field, and he has since been followed by many others. The Zero Point Field essentially is the energy left in a space when all other energy and matter are removed. This remaining field comprises, literally, a supercharged, sea-of-light backdrop to everything. Physicists have theorized that if we learn how to tap it, it could become a limitless energy supply, meeting all our current needs, even enabling Star Trek–like space travel. Well-known physicist Richard Feynman suggested "the energy in a single cubic meter of space is enough to boil all the oceans of the world."

As physicists work to explain and tap this incredible ocean of light, another very different glimpse into the light comes from the growing body of research of those who've had near-death experiences. Consistently, people who have clinically died and been revived tell a similar story of coming into contact with a mystical light. These experiences are profoundly transforming, leaving the survivors forever changed, with a measurably higher zest for life than the general population, more apt to have psychic abilities, and perhaps even more intelligent.

It could be that the brief clinical death releases these individuals from the limitations of physical perception and enables them to have a direct experience of the Zero Point Field. Interestingly, the mystical light people describe is far from cold or neutral. Again and again, those who've seen it tell of a Light that is powerfully benevolent, a Light of unconditional love. A limitless, living energy field of light and love, one that is everywhere yet is invisible to our physical senses—it sounds like a description of God.

Science writer and author of *The Field*, Lynne McTaggart, hinted at this benevolent, mystical nature of the universe in the summation of her excellent compilation of cutting-edge science. She suggests new scientific thinking promises to give us back our optimism as we realize we aren't simply alone in an indifferent universe. "Far from destroying God," she says, "science for the first time was proving His existence...."

The Zero Point Field

Spend today being aware of the Zero Point Field. Name it God, the Field, the Light, Holy Spirit, or anything you like. Imagine it as a wholly benevolent, loving energy that fills and surrounds you. There is no place this energy isn't. Look up from these words for a moment and imagine the invisible air around you filled with energy that has intelligence and potential. Feel the very air around you to be alive and holding you in a loving embrace. Relax into it. 🦋 🦋 🦋

Now look around in your space and imagine you can see the invisible light that permeates the physical realm. Objects that once looked dense and inanimate are now radiant and alive with the energy of love. 🦋 🦋 🦋

Look at your body and realize it, too, is infused with energy that loves you. With each breath you take, imagine breathing in a wise and benevolent energy that loves you. 🦋 🦋 🦋

As you go about your day, imagine walking through this energy of radiant light that loves you, holds you, and wants only the best for you. Each time you become aware of it, you relax. 🦋 🦋 🦋

If you'd like to take the exercise further, play with the energy and see what it does. Move it with your hands and imagine making light ripples. Blow it out your mouth in a stream of love to your pet, a plant, or a person across the street. *Don't try to change anyone with this energy. Give it unconditionally.* Concentrate a ball of it between your hands, and place it on your body where you have an ache or pain. Aim a beam of it as light out through your heart, your eyes, or even your toes to anyone you'd like to unconditionally bless. See what else you can do with it.

9
Tapping the Field

SCIENTISTS ARE WORKING ON MACHINES to extract energy from the limitless Zero Point Field and may someday succeed, but perhaps there is a more commonplace path into the Field—one accessible to all of us. If, as near-death accounts suggest, unconditional love is synonymous with the sea-of-light underpinnings of the universe and, if what religions refer to as "God" has some corollary in the Zero Point Field, maybe tapping the field happens naturally as we practice unconditional love and open ourselves to the sacredness of life.

I was introduced to the concept of unconditional love in my earliest metaphysics classes as a teenager. I heard that "We are love," and I was instructed to "Fill myself with love," or "Send unconditional love." I had no idea what any of this meant. But it did start me noticing what I felt when I used the word *love*. I found whether it was an intimate acquaintance, a piece of music, or a great dessert I "loved," the experience was invariably pleasurable and expansive. It brought my attention to the present moment and I felt more alive, uplifted, less distracted by life's trivial concerns.

Of course, addictions are born when we believe we can't have this alive and pleasurable moment without the external catalyst, be it more of our beloved or more dessert. Addictions are all about more. When we think of what we're addicted to, we feel empty and crave more. When we think about what we love, we feel full.

What Can Fill You at the Very Thought?

Who and/or what in your life do you love in a way that the very thought of that person or thing fills you up? Read this part slowly. Let memories come up and allow time to savor them. Can you recall a perfect moment of love between you and a beloved, a child, a friend, a family member, a pet? Or a most beautiful day in nature where nothing exists but the pleasure of the sounds, the smells, the views, and the air on your skin? Perhaps a perfect experience of art or music or some other kind of savoring? Maybe a time you laughed so hard, you cried. Or a sublime and peaceful moment with God.

Can you bring this moment to mind so clearly that the pleasure of it is literally with you now so you are purely in the moment and feeling more alive and content than you were just minutes ago? If so, your thoughts are having a very real and healthy effect on your physical body functions, and you are possibly doing exactly what physicists haven't figured out how to do: tapping the limitless energy of the Zero Point Field.

The more we cultivate these moments of love, the more we amplify good in our lives. I know a woman who helped herself recover from a serious bout of illness by looking at pictures of baby animals every day, simply because they triggered for her this powerfully healing experience of love. Dean Ornish, M.D., in his excellent book, *Love and Survival*, pulled together decades of medical research documenting the connection between physical healing and all different forms of love, whether from the impersonal touch of a nurse taking blood pressure, interactions with friends and community, or the experience of stroking a pet. He concludes that "love and intimacy are among the most powerful factors in health and illness." Quite simply, every time we experience even an instant of unconditional love, inner peace, compassion, and forgiveness, we're in a powerful healing state.

If it was difficult to find anything in your memories that could fill you simply at the thought—which can happen when we're feeling at a low point in life or if we've had a long history of depression or disappointment—the way into these moments of fullness is through imagination. When we feel empty, we tend to use our imagination to envision and amplify everything we lack. Imagination is such a powerfully creative tool, that when we use it in the service of emptiness, we dig ourselves into a deeper hole of scarcity. But imagination can also take us to wonderful places that life experience hasn't.

Putting imagination to work in the service of love means, not just envisioning the circumstances we want to happen, but cultivating the inner experiences we want in life. Too much emphasis on envisioning outcomes can amplify attachment, leaving us more concerned about the future than feeling content in the present. The inner experiences that fill us up in the moment, however, connect us to the Field and attract the outcomes that match the joy we've created within (often better outcomes than we could imagine).

The following is an experiment in using the power of imagination and love to tap the Zero Point Field. For best results, do this experiment in a quiet, reflective state of mind when you have some time to yourself.

Experiment
Tapping the Field

> Relax your body and quiet your thoughts with some deep, slow breaths. ❦ ❦ ❦ Imagine the clear, bright energy of other readers, past, present, and future, joining you. We are all vibrating together now in shared consciousness beyond the illusionary limits of space and time, each of us bringing only higher love to the whole. See this joining as beautiful, sacred, awe-inspiring, and filled with the potent energy of love.

As a group, we form a powerful network for healing and miracles. Recognize how much more powerful we are together. Our joined intentions quicken our growth, awaken our intuition, and heighten our magnetism to our highest good. What has seemed difficult in the past will come more easily now. Take a moment to feel the light and energy of the network building. ❦❦❦

Now we're going to expand our access to the Zero Point Field—to God energy. So for this, allow some of the most perfect moments of love that you've experienced to come to mind, moments of love so powerful you feel filled and content in the moment just by recalling them. And if you can't think of any such moments, it's okay to recall moments that haven't happened yet in linear time. Imagine loving life so much you can't wait to jump out of bed in the morning and to sleep at night feeling grateful and content, looking forward to the following day simply because life is good. You don't have to fill in the details of why. ❦ ❦ ❦

Imagine the most perfect day in nature where your mind becomes quiet and you can't help but become one with the beauty around you. Perhaps you're in an exquisite garden on the sunniest day with flowers everywhere, fragrance in the air, birds singing, the very air charged with peace. And you breathe it in; you soak in it, absorbing beauty through your very pores. All you can feel is joy and gratitude. ❦ ❦ ❦

Imagine now the inspiration, the reverence, the savoring of a fine work of art or music that lifts you out of yourself, beauty that touches your heart and soul, and moves you to the core. Or think of the experience of being in a spiritually charged, sacred place or in the midst of a spiritual experience, with the presence of God palpable and awe-inspiring, and you give yourself over to it. ❦ ❦ ❦

Now, imagine melting into the loving embrace of someone you love dearly who loves you just as much. You don't need to know who; you might be remembering someone you haven't met yet). Relax into the deep comfort that comes when love, trust, and familiarity are all present. Feel the joy when chemistry and compatibility are there. Imagine sharing laughter that just won't stop or be controlled and sleeping peacefully at night because life is good and you are loved. 🦋 🦋 🦋

Imagine holding a small child, a kitten, puppy, or other tiny creature, who relaxes into you with complete trust. Feel how soft and sweet the little body is against you and how unconditionally this small being loves. Imagine loving so deeply that tears come.

Take a moment to simply enjoy whatever experiences of love most touch you, heart and soul. 🦋 🦋 🦋

And now, imagine the energy of the Zero Point Field. Picture it as a field all around you and within you, an ever-present, invisible sea of light containing unlimited potential. What's more, it is inherently intelligent and kind. Feel the very air around you to be alive and filled with love. Feel it holding you in an intimate embrace, just like those loving arms of a beloved embracing you as you had imagined earlier. Relax completely and softly into this loving energy, just like a small child filled with absolute trust. 🦋 🦋 🦋

Now you've tapped the Field. This energy is having a very real effect on you, body and mind. If you're in need of healing, this will give you a boost. Don't try to focus on anything; just be the tiny child, completely relaxed in loving arms. Don't be surprised if you start noticing more and more that life is good.

Let this feeling of relaxing into the goodness of life reach a peak of intensity, and send it to all those others who have read, are reading, and will read these words. Your directed love is an invisible, yet very real and powerful, force. It's quietly helping to make life better for someone, for many, whom you will never meet. Realize that some have already sent this gift of grace to you and their love is quietly making life better for you. You are more loved than you know.

10
The Miracle Rose

JUST FIVE DAYS BEFORE I WAS SCHEDULED TO LEAVE
for a month-long healing and seminar tour of Europe, my
husband called from work and asked me to pick him up, as
he wasn't feeling well. I struggled not to panic as he described
stroke-like symptoms of losing function in his hand and leg. I
rushed out the door, and within twenty minutes we were on
our way to the emergency room. With one hand on the steering
wheel and one hand on him, I calmed myself by going into a
familiar healing state.

Once we were in the emergency room, an MRI test was quickly
scheduled to scan his brain. The medical team asked Bill
repeatedly if he was claustrophobic since the test involved a
forty-minute wait in a narrow tube, and he said it wouldn't be a
problem. But once in the MRI, he panicked almost immediately
and couldn't go through with it. Up to this point, we had both
been very calm and adult in the face of our first serious health
crisis, but for Bill, the MRI brought up the full, terrifying impact
of living the rest of his life in decline with a serious health
condition. Normally a rock under pressure, he broke down in a
way I had never seen before, and he came very close to leaving
the emergency room. We were left alone together for a couple of
hours to decide what to do.

I kept my hands on him, channeling healing energy as he agonized over the decision. At one point I felt a shift from the hot, physical healing energy I associate with emergency care to a more refined vibration I experience as Mother Mary energy. The visual image that comes to me with this energy is of Mother Mary and a fully opened, mandala-like rose. Just as this energy and visual came to me, Bill opened his eyes and said, "I see a rose!" He thought it was me he was experiencing but I explained it was the Mary energy coming through. Shortly afterward, Bill was calm enough to successfully complete the MRI, which did in fact, show he'd had a small stroke.

The next day our close friends came to the hospital to visit and brought the gift of a miniature rose in a small vase. They didn't know about our experience with the healing rose but their rose was exactly the color, shape, and full-blown bloom of the one we both had seen. Their rose gift came from a very special rose bush that had all but died before being carefully nursed back to life by our friend Ravyn.

Bill named it the miracle rose, and his recovery was equally miraculous. His stroke had occurred late on a Friday afternoon, and by Sunday he left the hospital with more than a 99-percent return of function. He was up and about on Monday, and by Tuesday he walked to work as usual. Not only is he still able to perform as a professional musician, but he noticed a slight increase of function in the hand that was affected.

Since Bill was well enough, I was able to leave for Europe a few days later without concern. During the month I was away, the miracle rose experience continued for both of us. While leading a seminar in Poland, I watched the group experience a particularly poignant moment when everyone lifted into healing simultaneously. An ordinary plaster statue of Mother Mary placed on a table behind me by the students seemed to add her comment by releasing a powerful scent of rose. As students noticed the fragrance, they ran to the statue to watch tears running down her cheeks and onto the paper placed carefully beneath her to catch the precious, scented drops. This was one of several, once ordinary now sacred, statues handled by a well-known Polish psychic surgeon who helped organize the seminar.

His students, who made up the class, were familiar with and delighted by this miraculous phenomenon. I, however, was still skeptical. Was I sure no one had slipped behind me to place a bit of oil on the Holy Mother? It wasn't until the next seminar when two of the crying statues were placed behind me where no one could gain access, that I finally acknowledged the miracle. Again I noticed waft after waft of rose scent. It was not a subtle "Did you smell that?" aroma, but a scent so heavy it drove a few people to the windows for fresh air. The scent recurred as though timed perfectly to the big moments of open-heartedness and high healing, and I couldn't help but relax into the simple miracle of God showing Herself to us as we opened ourselves to Her. I was given one of the statues to take home with me.

Bill took the tiny rose in its vase home from the hospital and kept it. Three weeks later, while I was having these amazing experiences in Poland, he sent me a picture of his rose, still completely fresh and intact—pretty amazing to anyone who knows the usual shelf life of cut roses. As the bloom finally did wither, the stem grew roots, new leaves, and even budded anew. The miracle rose became a miracle rose bush, which we still have in our home.

Experiment
Your Miracle Rose

During this European trip, while I was doing private healing sessions, I often felt the presence of roses. With one individual in particular, I was guided to suggest to her that roses would be showing up in her life in miraculous ways, as a sign that something wonderful is afoot. She said, "Yes! That has already been happening," and recounted beautiful stories of roses serendipitously showing up in connection with fortunate events.

As I write these words, I once again feel the familiar Divine Mother energy and see the mandala rose of Her healing grace. With all my love, I send it forward in time to all of you who are now reading these words. 🦋 🦋 🦋 Expect to see signs of this Divine Love showing up for you in the form of roses!!

This week (and longer, if you like), allow roses to come into your life. They may come in pictures, in fresh blooms, in words, or works of art. You may just notice the scent of roses where you don't even see any flowers. Receive each gift of roses as a manifestation of Divine Grace and a sign that wonderful things are afoot. Expect serendipity and give thanks every time it occurs.

To keep the blessing of roses growing, every time you experience roses coming to you, imagine sending them to every reader, past, present, and future. Picture miracle roses blessing with grace and serendipity all these souls with whom you are now deeply connected in love.

// Bending Time

CONSIDER THAT WHEN YOU'RE RUNNING LATE you could expand time to make more of it. Imagine being able to heal an illness in the past, right at its inception, instead of at its current, more advanced state. We'll experiment with this in Chapter 24.) Suppose you could condense time and skip steps that lie between where you are now and a desired future outcome (as subatomic particles are known to do when they make quantum leaps). Or imagine being able to simply send a state of mind, such as joy, into the future so it will be there waiting for you.

These concepts aren't as far out as they seem. Einstein proved in his theory of relativity that time and space aren't fixed and neutral containers for the material world; rather, they can be altered by what they contain. And there's already a significant body of research demonstrating that intention can change the past. Science writer Lynne McTaggart, who documents much of this research in her book, *The Intention Experiment*, writes, "...we believe that the consequences of our intentions can occur only in the future. What we do today cannot affect what happened yesterday. However, a sizeable body of the scientific evidence about intention violates these basic assumptions about causation."

A handful of folks in my weekly class did some experimenting with time and discovered that expanding it to avoid being late is actually quite easy. If you'd like to try this yourself, here's an exercise. For best results, I recommend practicing the following visualization a few times before you're in a situation when you need it, so it'll come more naturally when you're actually running late and need a few extra minutes.

Exercise
Expanding Time When You're Running Late

Bring to mind the experience of what it's like to run late. Notice what you usually do: the thoughts you think, what you feel, the stress that builds up in your body. Let the experience become very real. 🦋 🦋 🦋

As you feel everything speeding up inside of you, winding tighter and tighter, stop the process, and let yourself become completely still. Relax. Let your shoulders drop. Stop thinking of where you're going and what you're doing. Just let go. 🦋 🦋 🦋 This may feel opposite to what you're conditioned to do, but let yourself do it anyway. Create a vivid inner experience of peace. If you're telling yourself you don't feel peaceful, and therefore can't call it to mind, invite your imagination to show you what it would be like if you did feel peace. Recall a time when you felt peaceful. Imagination will take us anywhere, even to the places we've never been and have no memory to draw upon.

Now imagine the universal fabric around you bending and flowing, reshaping itself to reflect your inner state of peace. Imagine time itself becoming soft and flexible and stretching to accommodate your needs. Hold a strong certainty that you now have plenty of time. Picture yourself being where you need to be on time, getting done what you need to do with time to spare, not needing to rush, or sacrifice, or feel stressed. Be light, playful, and peaceful as you imagine these things. Let it be a game and not deadly serious. Let go of any attachment you may have to the outcome so it no longer matters whether you have enough time or not. Affirm everything will work out perfectly no matter what, and that there's plenty of time.

Continue what you were doing, maintaining this light, peaceful, state of mind. See if you don't wind up with time to spare!

Exercise
Sending Peace Forward in Time to an Important Event

This exercise is particularly useful for those situations you expect to be stressful, such as important meetings, emotionally charged family gatherings, or situations that test your performance in some way. Bring to mind an upcoming event you want to go well. Begin by noticing what thoughts and feelings come up as you anticipate the event—then stop the process. ❦ ❦ ❦ Stop thinking about what's going to happen and just be still. Relax, let your shoulders drop, your jaw relax, your stomach muscles soften. ❦ ❦ ❦ Take some deep, slow breaths, and simply be present in the moment, letting every part of you relax. As with the first exercise, create the inner experience of peace. When you are deeply peaceful and relaxed, add to this inner state any other feelings you want to have in this future situation: confidence, love, competence, victory, joy, whatever best fits.

When you feel everything you want to feel in this future event, imagine sending your inner state forward in time. Imagine time as a linear path, streaming endlessly behind you and before you. Envision where this important date falls on the timeline, and either project a fluid energy wave of all your good feelings forward to this point in time, or imagine time condensing so the distance between the present and the future disappears. Imagine this moment and the future moment overlapping. Now you can infuse the future with the power of your peaceful inner state. When you feel completely at peace in this future event, let it go, and come back to the present moment.

Let go of any attachment you may have to the outcome of this occasion. Know that your state of peace is drawing to you whatever outcomes best serve the highest good of all, and everything will work out perfectly no matter what.

———•———

What if we could plant a reminder of peace and well-being to go off within us everyday like an internal alarm clock? What if we've already sent such a reminder to ourselves from the future? Could this reminder have radically shaped our past in ways we may never fully comprehend? Summing up some of the amazing research on time, Lynn McTaggart concludes in *The Intention Experiment,* "It may well be that every action we take, every thought we have in the present, alters our entire history." Time research seems to be creating more questions than it answers. For this next experiment, though, let go of the questions and just be open to the possibilities. For best results, do the following in a quiet, reflective state of mind when you have some uninterrupted time to yourself.

Experiment
2 p.m.

Relax your body and quiet your thoughts with some deep, slow breaths. 🦋 🦋 🦋 Let your attention relax deeply into the present moment, and become aware of the limitless, loving energy of the Zero Point Field all around you. You may notice that, with each experiment, it gets easier to tap this beautiful God energy. Let it wash through you, lighting up every cell in your body, filling you with profound peace and well-being. 🦋 🦋 🦋

See the clear, bright energy of other readers, past, present, and future, joining you. We are all vibrating together now in shared consciousness beyond the illusionary limits of space and time, each of us bringing only higher love to the whole. See this joining as beautiful, sacred, and filled with the potent energy of love. The connection to other readers amplifies your own experience of peace and well-being, like turning a dimmer switch up to full power.

Picture the network of all of us as a joy-filled web of light. ❦ ❦ ❦ Now bring to mind the linear time line of the future and envision 2 p.m.—every 2 p.m. every day from now on. Send a big, collective burst of joy, from the whole network to every 2 p.m. from now on for every person in this group. Send it forward in time so every 2 p.m. from now on is infused with the sweetness of life. As you send this to everyone in our network of readers, feel their joy at having daily reminders that life is good. Hold the intention that every 2 p.m. from now on has the collective energy of the whole group mind so it will go off like a powerful cellular alarm clock, reawakening our connection to limitless God energy.

After sending it forward, send this burst of joy backward in time to every 2 p.m. for yourself and every reader. Send it back so every 2 p.m. you've ever lived through was filled with potential, whether you recognized it or not; every 2 p.m. was a whisper that led you to this moment.

Do this lightly, without attachment to outcomes, and then let it go. Don't try to understand what effect this is having on your past. Just trust that it is, and don't try to guess what effect this will have on your future. Just know that it will. There's nothing more you need do around this. Just start noticing 2 p.m.

Question for Thought

Now that you've read this chapter, your every 2 p.m. has become full rather than neutral. You can't lose it or undo it anymore than you can "unthink" an elephant. Imagine people from the past sending joy into your 2 p.m. Imagine people from the future sending joy into your 2 p.m. What do you imagine you could do with 2 p.m. now that it will never be quite the same?

12

What Do You Want?

WHAT IS IT THAT YOU MOST WANT? And how often do you even stop to ask yourself this question? Desiring from life isn't a selfish thing. Desire is a way inner guidance speaks to us about our path of highest good. Our true heart's desires always lead us to love: love of self, love for all creation, and the awareness that there is no difference in these because we're all one. There is a harmony, a divine order, in following our heart's desires. Our heart's desires bring personal joy and inner peace and allow us to make a contribution to the whole. What may look like a frivolous and purely selfish desire—say, a craving for a long beach vacation—may be just what's needed to birth a new creative vision that ultimately will serve many. When we're acting on our true desires, not our addictions, they lead us where we need to go, even if we don't completely understand *how* at the time.

Yet our true heart's desires can be elusive, covered over by years of disappointment, feelings of unworthiness, fear that there's not enough of anything good to go around, and learned habits of resignation that tell us we can't get what we want so we may as well settle for what we can get. Then we turn to numbing habits of addiction to fill the void left by the absence of our heart's desire. We overeat, overwork, abuse alcohol and drugs. When we fill our lives with things that don't fulfill us, we further separate ourselves from what we truly need and we undermine our power to get it.

Dreaming and desiring can foster creativity and keep us aligned with our path of highest good. It's difficult to create what we're not willing to imagine. Once we imagine something, though, even if we imagine it as impossible, we've taken the first step in making it real.

Manifesting a Home

I quite unexpectedly manifested a home this way. For several years I lived in a cramped apartment in a very beautiful, large building I had bought with my friend Kathleen. The manifestation of this property happened very miraculously shortly after Kathleen and I decided we wanted to buy an apartment building together. Just several weeks after forming our intent, the building was practically gifted to us by Kathleen's landlady, who sold it to us, along with a small condo unit next door, so far under market value that we were able to secure a mortgage without using any of our own funds. I've always been grateful for it—even when I was uncomfortable in my too-small apartment! When another friend of mine decided to sell one of his rental properties, I stopped by to see it, thinking I'd help spread the word for him. As I walked through the bright, spacious, newly renovated upper unit of the duplex, I found myself imagining what I'd do with that much space. I wasn't financially in a place to buy the building, so I knew I was just daydreaming. I even checked the financials and confirmed it was too much money. But still, I couldn't stop imagining myself living there. My "daydreams" weren't fraught with longing; they were light and fun. I would find myself mentally placing my furniture in the new space and enjoying the new arrangement.

Over the next month, my real estate circumstances took some unexpected turns. For reasons unrelated to the duplex, Kathleen and I decided to sell rather than rent our small condo unit next door and, to our surprise, we wound up selling it for far more than we had paid for it several years earlier. Suddenly we had a lot of cash! What's more, my friend kept dropping the price on his duplex until it became a much smarter purchase. The price was right, the money was there, and the deal happened. Kathleen and I were able to purchase another property together without touching a cent of our personal finances, I had the living space I wanted, and all I did to make it happen was imagine.

Exercise
Write Down Your Heart's Desires

Give some time and attention to dreaming about what you want in life, and describe all of your heart's desires. See if you can identify anywhere from one to several heart's desires for all the important areas of life you can think of. I've included a worksheet (see page 61) with categories to help you get started. Or you can simply write a detailed description of the life you would like to be living, in the present tense, as though it's already happening. Include in your write-up only your goals, not process steps.

Goals are outcomes that would fill us with joy and fulfillment to do, be, or have. A process step is an action that we think will lead to the fulfillment of a goal. For example, if radiant health is the goal, making dietary changes, starting an exercise program, and going to the doctor are process steps that may lead to the outcome of radiant health. If you make these process steps into goals without the clear intention of radiant health behind them, you may successfully accomplish all of these and, in the end, still not have radiant health. What's more, accomplishing these process-step goals won't bring you joy. You'll feel like you worked hard for nothing. When you identify the true goal—that is, the outcome that will fill you with joy at its fulfillment—you may not have to do as many steps as you think. You might find yourself drawn to the right health practice or practitioner that's just what you need, and because it's the right fit, you'll be more motivated to do what's needed to be healthy. Or you might find that your attention is drawn away from health altogether, and you heal spontaneously while pursuing a new and gratifying career path.

Process steps do not, in and of themselves, fill us with joy, although when our goals are truly in alignment with our heart, we're more likely to undertake process steps joyfully. For example, I wouldn't enjoy a career in advertising, yet when I'm excited about a new project, I undertake the work of advertising it with enthusiasm.

As you create your Heart's Desires List, be aware that simply identifying and writing your goals start the manifestation process. It's directing unconscious creative power toward your desires, making you more magnetic to them. I often give the assignment in my workshops to create a heart's desires list and can't even count all the folks who've reported back to me in just a few months that most of their list had already materialized. With that in mind, put all of your joy and excitement into this list!

The Path to Success Sometimes Looks Like Failure

Do be aware, however, that because of the limited vision of our personality, the path to success can sometimes look like failure for a time. For example, at one time, I had my own church. It was a small, fledgling organization, and I prayed for it to grow bigger. However, the more energy I put into growing it bigger, the smaller it got. While I was up to my neck in the time-consuming work of building an organization, I was recruited to take a ministerial position at a well-established independent New Thought church. My reason counseled me against it: I was already too busy with one church, so what did I need with another?! But, without quite knowing why, or even wanting the position, I accepted.

Very quickly, I realized this was the answer to my prayers. Rather than growing my own church bigger, taking on all the administrative work of an expanding organization, my Higher Self, who was wiser, opened the door for me to work in an already bigger church—one that didn't need me to oversee the administration. It offered a number of other perks as well, such as the support of working with peers. This latter was something I didn't realize how much I needed until I had it. Spirit provided the perfect answer to my prayers, and I had to be willing to give up my attachment to my own vision in order to receive it. So, no matter what you imagine to be your highest heart's desire, consider there might be something even better that you just haven't dreamed yet.

Heart's Desires List

Work/Creative Expression

_____

_____

Money/Material Possessions

_____

_____

Romance/Partnership

_____

_____

Family

_____

_____

Friends

_____

_____

Health/Body Image

_____

_____

Home

_____

_____

Recreation

_____

_____

Spirituality

_____

_____

State of Mind

_____

_____

Other

_____

_____

13

Spontaneous Manifestation? Easier Than You Think!

I ONCE WITNESSED A POLISH HEALER, the same fellow whose plaster statues of Mary are prone to weeping real rose oil tears, work on someone, and at the end of the session reach both hands up in the air as if waiting to catch something. I found out later that his inner guidance had informed him that "medication" was coming. His sleeves were rolled up past his elbows (nothing up his sleeve), and I was standing just a few feet away, so I could see everything very clearly. I saw him bring his hands down, roll his fingers together, and there in his fingers was a small, bright red capsule, which he gave to his patient with the instruction to take it the next day at 7 p.m.

This, Mother Mary's tears, and new dental fillings appearing instantaneously as a healer works are all examples of spontaneous manifestation. Perhaps it's difficult to personally relate to the experiences of a small handful of healers, but here's a story closer to everyday. It was told to me by a young woman in one of my workshops who I knew to be of very high integrity and honesty, so I believed her. She received, in the workshop, the gift of a beautiful coral bead from another participant. The young woman later shared a very startling experience she'd had with the bead. First she dreamed that it had a small crystal in its hollow center and then, after meditating with the bead in her hand, she opened her eyes to find that a small crystal had materialized in its center, just as in her dream.

The quantum corollary for this type of manifestation is the quantum leap, in which subatomic particles materialize spontaneously out of the energy soup underpinnings of the material world, leaping from one point to another without passing through the points in between.

While rose oil tears, red pills, and crystals from thin air are dramatic examples, most of us have probably had experiences of thinking of something and then having it show up in our physical surroundings in a highly coincidental way rather than through any intentional actions on our part.

Matter is tremendously responsive to our thoughts and, while it's still more or less ignored by the bulk of the scientific community, a large body of research documents the power of consciousness to affect matter. As early as the 1960s, research physicist Helmut Schmidt conducted many experiments on the mind-matter connection with convincing positive evidence. In spite of the credibility of his research, his work tended to be categorized as parapsychology and dismissed as a fringe science.

In the 1970s, Robert Jahn, dean of Princeton University's school of engineering, in spite of his initial skepticism, became intrigued with Schmidt's work through one of his undergraduate students. In pursuing his own work in this area, Jahn steered clear of the marginalizing labels of the paranormal, bringing to his research the prestigious backing of Princeton University and a rigorous grounding in traditional science. He partnered with developmental psychologist Brenda Dunne, and the two of them went on to collect many years worth of data showing irrefutably that human will alone can affect the random movement of machines. Not only human will—they also found that baby chicks and bunnies could call a robot to themselves once the machine had been imprinted upon thei from birth, and they had attached to it as a mother. Other interesting results showed that bonded pairs of people could affect the random mechanism of a machine six times more powerfully than single operators could, thus demonstrating the synergy of harmoniously joined consciousness.

Manifestation, however, is something more than telekinesis, which involves moving an object already present. Manifesting is the art of drawing to us something (or materializing it out of thin air) that isn't present, which is what we'll practice in the next exercise. For this exercise, you will picture a small object in your hand and use your imagination to make it real. Then you'll forget about it and let the object show up in your life. It's a simple and very easy exercise to help you demonstrate to yourself the power of your consciousness.

The first time I did this myself, I imagined a large, polished stone in my hand. I pictured a size and shape of stone I hadn't seen before, and I didn't have a lot of faith that this would work. However, within days, I found my stone in a cluttered store. It didn't have a price marked on it and, when I took it to the register to buy, the proprietress was perplexed, because she didn't recall ever seeing the stone before!

The second time I did this exercise in a workshop I was leading. I immediately pictured an eagle feather in my hand. As this went against my own instruction not to pick something terribly rare (I couldn't imagine spontaneously happening upon an eagle feather), I changed my object to a seagull feather.

Immediately following the workshop, I had an appointment to receive a healing session. The healer had a playfully flamboyant style and brought out a number of beautiful and sacred objects in preparation for our healing. When we were nearly ready, almost as an afterthought, she asked, "Do you think we'll need an eagle feather?" I was electrified by her words and said, "Yes, I think so!" She brought out a beautiful golden eagle feather, a prized possession gifted to her by a friend. She performed the healing using the feather as a wand and I was delighted. I couldn't imagine coming across an eagle feather at all, let alone within hours of envisioning it, but there it was!

Still another time I did this exercise I pictured hummingbird feathers. This time it took many months before my feathers came to me, yet when they did, it was as an unexpected gift presented to me right before the first Sunday service I ever led as an ordained minister. The timing was definitely right.

When I've led this exercise in my workshops, I've often seen people manifest their objects before leaving the room. So, have fun with this and be light about it. It may amaze you with its speedy fulfillment or it may require more time for the synchronicity of the message to be exactly right. Either way, trust it's in process.

This is best done with eyes closed, so either read it and then practice it, make a recording that you can listen to, or have someone read it to you.

Exercise
Easy Manifesting

Close your eyes, relax, and take a few deep breaths. ❦ ❦ ❦ As your body relaxes, let your attention turn inward and your mind become quiet. ❦ ❦ ❦ Think of a material object you would like to manifest, one small enough to fit in your hand. Make it something that has a pleasant feeling to it—something you'd like to have in your hand: a useful object, a beautiful object, something you want, but not something that has a strong emotional charge to it, as with something very rare or precious. Let it be an object you have warm feelings about, but not one you feel especially attached to having. Choose something you don't already own or have easy access to.

Now picture this object in your hand. Use your imagination to make it completely real and solid in your hand. See it there. Feel it. Pass it from one hand to the other. Touch it to your tongue.

Sniff it. Create a feeling of certainty that this imaginary reality is now calling forth the physical reality of this object in your hand. Feel happy and certain about this.

Then let it go, keeping only a pleasant feeling of well-being and accomplishment. Imagine that when this object shows up in your life, it's a signal some aspect of your highest good is unfolding. Now forget about it. Really forget about it.* It will come when the time is right. Complete your visualization with another deep breath and open your eyes.

---

*One woman forgot the exercise so completely that it wasn't until after she found her object in a shop, bought it, brought it home, and had it in her possession for a time that she remembered it was exactly what she had seen in her visualization!

14

Manifesting Your Heart's Desires

ARE YOU READY NOW TO MANIFEST your deepest heart's desires? You don't need to be free of doubts, just ready, willing, and unattached to the outcome. The most successful result may match none of your expectations, as you'll see in the story that follows! It would be helpful to have completed a list or written description of your heart's desires, as the chapter 12 exercise instructs, before going on. As I've mentioned before, simply writing down what you want is a creative act, and by writing your list, you may have already experienced things from your list showing up in your life by one means or another. Giving attention to the list, as we will do next, further fuels the manifesting process.

Be light and playful about this experiment, yet understand how potent this work is. We have a powerful added ingredient here in the amplifying effect of many minds joined in a common intent. Every time you have performed one of the experiments in this book, imagining a loving connection with other readers across space and time, you have added energy to the group mind. When you or someone else brings this benevolent, helpful pool of consciousness to mind, it becomes stronger for everyone and easier for each individual to access. Because intention can flow forward and backward in time, it becomes possible for you to benefit from loving thoughts sent back in time by future readers who haven't even heard of this book yet!

If this latter idea seems too big a stretch to take seriously, consider this: the aforementioned research team Robert Jahn and Brenda Dunne, who are just two of many researchers finding evidence that intention can travel backward in time, actually noticed greater effects in their time-displaced trials than in their standard present-time experiments. Theirs and other research raise the interesting possibility that intention might flow even more powerfully outside the parameters of time and space as we think of them.

Your Heart's Desires Might Not Take the Form You Expect

All this is to help you recognize how potentially life-changing these experiments are. For best results, go into this next one with an expectancy that anything—yes, *anything*—is possible, and an awareness that none of your heart's desires may take the form you think. Trust that even what looks like obvious failure is a step in the direction of your highest success.

Here's a perfect example of this—and the surprising story I hinted at in the chapter's opening. Once in a workshop in preparation for a healing exercise, I asked people to form an intention for what they most wanted to heal and/or manifest. One man wanted a painful plantar wart on his foot to disappear. After everyone had identified something, I asked them to think of something even bigger. This man decided that what he really wanted was "a better relationship with Kathy," his wife. Immediately after the healing circle, his wart disappeared completely but his relationship with Kathy painfully disintegrated, and soon they were divorcing. The lesson he took from this was that he should have just settled for the wart going away and not asked for more. But then, about a year and a half later, he was attending another group session with me and recalling his miraculous healing of the plantar wart, when suddenly it dawned on him that, even though his marriage had ended, he was now sitting next to his new girlfriend, also named Kathy! He had, in fact, manifested "a better relationship with Kathy," just not in the way he had envisioned.

The following is best done in a quiet state of mind when you have some uninterrupted time to yourself.

Experiment
Our Hearts' Desires

Relax your body and quiet your thoughts with some deep, slow breaths. ❦ ❦ ❦ Let your sense of identification shift so that, instead of feeling yourself to be defined by your physical body, separate, and dense, you become aware of yourself as clear, bright, beautiful energy. Through this simple shift in perception, you leave behind the limitations of dense matter and start to vibrate in the unlimited way of light, energy, and love. Feel the very cells of your physical body becoming less dense, the molecules, the atoms, the subatomic particles spreading out, vibrating in love and light. You're shifting from the limited paradigm of "particle" reality to the limitlessness of "wave" reality.*

See the bright energy of other readers, past, present, and future, joining you. We are all vibrating together now in joined consciousness beyond the illusionary limits of space and time, each of us bringing only higher love to the whole. Picture this joining in light and love in whatever way feels most powerful to you. You might imagine us all meeting in a magnificent, sacred arena in the spiritual realm or see us forming a wavelike circle of energy or network of light.

---

*For a fascinating firsthand description of this very experience by a brain scientist, check out some of the YouTube videos of Jill Bolte Taylor who speaks about the Nirvana-like experiences she had during a stroke that turned off the left hemisphere of her brain, leaving her to experience pure right-brain consciousness.

Manifesting Your Heart's Desires

See this joining as beautiful, sacred, awe-inspiring, and filled with the potent energy of love.

As a group, we form a powerful network for healing, support, and manifestation. Recognize how much more powerful we are together. Our joined intentions quicken our growth, awaken our intuition, and heighten our magnetism to our highest good. What has seemed difficult in the past will come more easily now. Take a moment to feel the light and energy of the network building. ₩ ₩ ᴡ

The light of our group is so bright now, we attract to us an even greater Light. Picture this as a brilliant spiritual sun shining light to all of us. Know this to be the Light of Divine Love—the essence of God—and feel it to be profoundly peaceful. Let it wash over you, through your body, as well as the energy field surrounding your body. This light shines away anything that has dimmed your radiance, and you see it burn away, melt away, wash away, or otherwise make disappear, wounds from the past, limiting beliefs, and whatever else you no longer need to carry in your body and mind.

As dis-ease is released and you fill with the deep peace of Divine Light, you become more powerfully radiant than you were before. In fact, each of us now emanates a more brilliant vibration of light. Our healing work has increased the energy available to our whole network of readers, preparing us all to receive our highest hearts' desires. It's not necessary that you be aware of all that's now happening in these invisible realms, but do be open to any impressions that come to you. You may have a wide range of visual, kinesthetic, auditory, olfactory, emotional, or inspirational experiences as spiritual reality breaks through into your conscious awareness.

Imagine that the hard, fixed nature of reality as you have known it is now becoming fluid and soft. "Cold, harsh reality" is an illusion of our own making and, as the illusion falls away, it's being replaced by something benevolent and responsive. It's into this reality, where all things are possible, that we will offer our Heart's Desires Lists.

Imagine, or actually hold, your list. See everyone in our network of readers doing the same. Take a moment to savor all the many life changes represented on your list. If there's one particularly important heart's desire, bring it to mind and step into it, imagining it as though it has already come to pass. 🦋 🦋 🦋 When you can feel the delight and fulfillment of your dreams manifest, let go of the pictures you have in mind, and just keep the good feeling.

Now, with all the lightness of being you can muster, imagine all of us, all at once, handing our desires up, letting them all fly free, each one becoming a butterfly. Enjoy the flurry of it as countless butterflies take flight, and send them off with the certainty that what comes back to you will be what you imagined or something better. Let your heart be filled with gratitude, giving thanks for all the blessings of your life—past, present, and future.

Enjoy this moment for as long as you like. When you're ready, complete your meditation by thanking all the souls in our network for their help. Take some deep full breaths and slowly come back to your normal waking state. As you return to an awareness of your physical body, come back feeling refreshed, every cell infused with health and vitality.

15
Surrender

NOW THAT WE'VE GIVEN LIFE to our human dreams
and desires, it's important to stop stressing and straining
to make them happen. Let go of trying to control the
outcome. Creating miracles, as opposed to simply manifesting
what we envision, isn't an exercise in imposing our intention
on the world around us. There are many books on visualization,
affirmation, treasure mapping, and other techniques for doing
just this. It's not that these techniques don't work. Invariably
they do work some of the time for some people. Sometimes the
results are dazzling and sometimes questionable. I once knew
a woman who practiced creative visualization to manifest a
new car. She envisioned the make, model, even the color, and
she did in fact, succeed in attracting a gift of just such a vehicle.
However, the gift came with no engine so she received it just as
she envisioned it—standing still!

Miracles aren't to be had in a structured, step-by-step way with
predictable results. They're more about allowing mystery into
the mix and trusting, not just our own agendas, but something
greater than ourselves. In keeping with this paradoxical nature
of miraculous experience, identifying what we desire needs
to go hand in hand with surrendering it all up to some Higher
Principle, freeing ourselves from desire and attachment in the
recognition that all we could ever possibly want is here now.

ut of the Fight

n't to be confused with giving up in defeat. It's
e battle; it's stepping out of the fight. There's an
exercise I sometimes do in workshops in which I work with
an individual who feels hopelessly stuck in some area of life.
I ask the "stuck" person to invite people from the group to
represent the various limiting messages she or he has going
on in their own head. These helpers externalize and dramatize
the person's inner dialogue, and what ensues is generally a
noisy debate between the protagonist and their "voices." At
some point in this drama, I ask the rest of the group to call to
the person, who's now locked in battle with their own demons,
to see if they can entice the person with offers of love and
kindness. It's fascinating to see how many people stubbornly
hang on to the fight and find it more compelling than the
breath of fresh air coming from beyond. There's never an end
to these battles. They could go on and on if I didn't intervene
and, even though fighting in the same old way doesn't
produce any new results, people keep at it as long as I let them.
When I do finally step in, the protagonist typically says, "Yup,
this is how I feel stuck in my life!"

Eventually, many in this exercise discover that, as much
as they hate the battle, it's energizing and seductively
holds their attention. Some realize that maintaining the
inner struggle feels comfortably familiar and safer than
being fully available to intimacy with other people and the
uncertainties of life. Those who break free from this inner
war don't do it by "winning"—they do it by losing interest in
it. They shift their attention from fighting what's wrong to
embracing love. The voices don't go away; they just fade into
the background and eventually wither from lack of attention.
This is the power of surrender. It requires letting go of
stubbornness, of being right, and of trying to control the
outcome. It requires stepping back from fighting whatever
condition we love to hate.

Trying Too Hard Leaves No Room for God to Intervene

Most of us are control freaks at heart. It's no wonder. The reality defined by our physical senses—the world comprised of what we can see and touch—often appears dangerous, made up of random forces beyond our control. It's easy to feel powerless and vulnerable and to respond by exercising as much control over our surroundings as we can. Miracle-making involves awakening to the reality that lies beyond the limits of our physical senses, realizing that we really do have the power to create our reality, and we're not at the mercy of a seemingly random universe.

Yet, to the extent that we feel alone in this creative process, we're still living from limitation. I've seen people take on the concept of creating their own reality as a terrible burden, planning, visualizing, and affirming every step of their lives, fearing that if they relax their discipline for a moment, they'll create the "wrong" reality. Paradoxically, as we recognize how powerful we really are, true power requires us to let go of control at times and to acknowledge our powerlessness in the face of God.

Ultimately, personal control—the power exercised at the personality level—isn't the same as true empowerment. The more we release attachment to our personal agendas and to specific outcomes, the more we naturally allow something higher and wiser than our personal will to lead. Accepting our powerlessness in the face of God is the humble recognition that the conscious personality we most often think of as our "self" is a limited tool, and to create something extraordinary, we sometimes need to set it down and give a rest to our need to push things forward.

Practices such as creative visualization or affirmations are only useful to the extent that we know what to affirm and visualize. Sometimes the limits of our imagination don't stretch wide enough to show us the true path of our highest good. It's when we use these methods to exercise rigid control over our lives that they backfire. When we try too hard, we may get what we ask for, but we don't get what we want. There comes a point when we need to trust in the process of life and give undreamed possibilities a chance to grow.

The researchers I've mentioned—Helmut Schmidt, as well as Robert Jahn and Brenda Dunne—found in their mind-controlling-matter experiments that many people were successful in influencing random effects in the *opposite* direction of their intention. In other words, their conscious minds were directing their subconscious power to cause an effect, but it was an effect of the subconscious mind's choosing—one that probably reflected performance fears, disbelief, and other agendas different from the conscious order to simply move forward. Too much conscious focus on making something happen can plug us into the fear-based energy of worry and attachment, triggering this subconscious, contrary response.

So, it's actually important to *stop* giving conscious attention to what you're manifesting at a certain point. Although conscious intent may steer the course, the energy for movement comes from the subconscious mind. It's a bit like turning a giant ship around in the ocean. The tiny captain in the enormous ship may have the idea to make the turn and the mechanism to accomplish it but he has to reckon with the huge force of the ship already set in motion. Our subconscious mind is much like the big ship already set on its path. Just as the captain needs to rely upon the ship's mechanism, not his own personal stressing and straining, to make the big ship turn, we need to allow what begins as a conscious intention to be handed over to the "engine" of our subconscious mind. This means knowing when to take our personal strength and will out of the process to let a bigger force than we can personally control take over.

I think of the perfect state of mind for manifesting as the one we bring to the experience of a most beautiful butterfly landing in our hand. We're still and focused, filled with joy and wonder. We're "holding" it, but with an open hand, willing to let it go. And when it flies away, we're left feeling full rather than empty.

So hold your heart's desires as you would a butterfly, not
raft clutched in fearful desperation. Surrender your plan
higher plan, and let it fly away. Even when it's out of sight
leave you feeling full and happy as you go about your day.

Questions for Thought

1. How are you pushing to know an outcome, or make a
   decision, or force something into being in a way that isn't
   really necessary at this time? See how many things you
   can think of that you're trying to push ahead that don't
   absolutely need to be acted upon or known right now.

2. What are you afraid would happen if you just let all these
   go for now?

Exercise
Take a Break from "Pushing"

Take a break from all the things you're pushing to know, to
decide, or to make happen, that don't have to be addressed
right now, especially those things that feel confusing and
aren't flowing easily. If you can't see a clear path between
where you are now and where you want to be, stop thinking
about it. Imagine that pushing ahead right now is like a
caterpillar trying to break out of its chrysalis before it's formed
into a butterfly, which will only result in birthing something
unformed. Imagine the part of you that's struggling to make
something happen is very small and has to step aside to allow
the hand of God to work its magic before you'll see the results
you want.

As you do this exercise, recognize that surrender is a state
of mind, not an action. Ultimately, it's a release of fear. It's
possible to stop what you're "doing" without achieving a state of
surrender. You also may find that as you achieve a surrendered
state, you are naturally led to many actions. What you are
releasing here is the "push" that's rooted in fear.

16

Making Each Moment Count

I KNOW A WOMAN WHO, AFTER BEING UNEMPLOYED for several years due to illness, decided it was time to work again. The prospect of finding an appropriate job that would interest her, use her creative skills, and accommodate the physical limitations she still had, seemed daunting. But rather than scouring the want ads, updating her resume, and going on endless job interviews, she devoted her attention to prayer. She focused on releasing her fear that she wouldn't find what she needed, and she imagined something wonderful showing up. She had a positive outcome in mind but she didn't cling to it, obsess on it, or worry about it. She held the intention just long enough to be clear and evoke a good feeling. Then she let it go. One day as she and I were out together, she felt compelled to stop and explore a small shop that neither of us had ever been in before. The store sold beautiful jewelry similar to what she herself made. Talking to the shop clerk, she discovered that much of the store's jewelry was made in a factory upstairs, and the shopkeepers were desperately in need of a new jeweler. She quickly applied and got the job. It satisfied her desire for challenging creative work, supportive co-workers, and flexible hours. She created all this purely through inner work and listening to her intuition when it guided her into the shop.

In the old model of the universe, the one made up of separate planet-sized, atom-sized, and human-sized particles, bringing something into physical manifestation requires forming a goal, then a plan, taking action, applying effort, going step by step, and following a linear route to an outcome. There's much waiting involved: waiting for the opportunity to take physical action, waiting for that action to bear fruit, waiting for our desired goal to make us happy. Consequently, our attention is often focused more on the future than the present.

When we begin to operate from the quantum model, in the realm too small to see, nothing is solid or fixed, and matter is responsive to thought, our state of mind rather than our physical actions becomes our more powerful tool. Therefore, our greatest power lies in the present moment, and there is no waiting because our state of consciousness is active and creative in every instant.

Simply living in the moment as fully and richly as possible is powerfully creative. This is when we experience miraculous coincidences and "lucky" breaks that are difficult to explain in the context of old-paradigm reality.

Exercise
Making the Most of the Present Moment

At least several times today, remind yourself that to create your highest possible future, all you need to do is release thoughts of the past and the future, and create this instant to be as full, rich, and loving as you would like the rest of your life to become.

With this thought, fill yourself for an instant with the inner experience of joy, love, and gratitude. Create this feeling so vividly that you experience it as a physical sensation of well-being in your body. Bring to mind any images that fill you with joy and peace, and say to yourself any words that help to trigger feelings of peace. ❦ ❦ ❦ When this inner experience reaches a peak of intensity, blow it out as a breath of perfect fulfillment to every reader in our network, past, present, and future. As you share it this way as an unconditional gift, feel it instantly come back to you as an amplified ripple of peace and well-being.

Realize that each instant devoted to fully experiencing the joy of life is a potent seed that is taking root and growing miracles. Don't worry if you don't stay in this instant for long. Don't try to hold the moment. Just return to it from time to time during the day.

17
Prayer

THERE'S A GROWING BODY OF RESEARCH documenting the powerful connection between prayer and healing.* Effects have been found even when the recipients don't believe in prayer or don't know that prayer is being said on their behalf. I've seen this myself in my prayer ministry. For more than a decade, I maintained a free service that allowed people to anonymously leave requests for healing prayer by phone or online.** The requests were sent to a group of people all over the country who prayed for them, at a distance sight unseen, every day. We received numerous reports of prayers being answered over the years, sometimes in quite dramatic ways, such as people showing up at the hospital for major surgery and finding they no longer needed it.

But for all the miraculous stories of prayers answered, there are just as many that don't get answered—which raises the question, why? What makes prayer work sometimes but not every time? Clearly I'm a believer in the power of prayer, but I also believe

---

*To delve more deeply into the science of prayer and the research behind it, Larry Dossey, MD, is one of the best known experts on this. His book, *Healing Words,* is a good starting place.

**At the time of this writing, my prayer ministry has evolved into a distance healing ministry in which a group of my trained healing ministers offer distance healing for all those who leave requests. To leave a request, go to www.lynnwoodland.com.

there's an art and science to it that make some prayers more potent than others.

For those of us who do turn to prayer in times of need, often we don't even think to ask God for help until we're in crisis and have exhausted all other resources. Perhaps we grew up thinking of God as an entity who could be bothered by our requests if they came too frequently or seemed too trivial. By the time we see fit to pray, our prayer come out as a desperate plea of "Pleeeaaassse God, rescue me!"

Or we may pray from our fear-based need for control and, instead of praying for the highest possible outcome, trusting God to show us what this is, we come to God with our grocery list of specific requests, saying, in effect, "This, God, and only this will do." Then we feel let down if God doesn't comply with our micromanaging. In this way, we undermine the power of prayer to give us what is truly for our highest good, not just for the best we can imagine.

Perhaps we'll try bartering: "Pleeeaaassse, God...I'll do anything!" affirming that our offering to God is conditional, at best. Desperation, micromanaging, and pitiful bartering aren't the most successful strategies for eliciting help from the people in our lives, and they don't work any better with God. These prayers are less a reflection of our trust in a benevolent universe and more an affirmation of our own powerlessness. The anger and loss of faith we feel when God doesn't come through on our terms leaves us feeling separate and alone, much the same way we feel when our friends don't respond to our fear-based manipulation.

Ask and You Will Receive

There's a Bible passage, Matthew 7:7, that reads, "Ask and you will receive; seek and you will find; knock and the door will be opened to you." I understand "Ask and you will receive" to be spiritual law, not religious metaphor, and, when applied correctly, it works absolutely. Not sometimes; every time.

Obviously there's a trick to it, because we all can name things we asked and pleaded for but never got. The secret lies in another spiritual law, which we've heard distorted in the familiar phrase "It's better to give than receive," but which comes through more clearly in the modern-day spiritual text *A Course in Miracles* as "Giving and receiving are the same."

If we combine "Ask and you will receive" with "Giving and receiving are the same," it means that to be truly effective, our request needs to offer up—to give unconditionally—a bit of what we're asking for. This is different from bartering in which we tell God, "If you give me everything I want, I'll give you my happiness! Really, I promise!" The kind of gift I'm referring to is one in which we give God our joy *now*, in absolute trust that whatever happens next will be just fine, whether it's as we envision or not.

A powerful prayer request is one in which we first create within ourselves a bit of the peace, joy, love, surrender, safety, and fulfillment we want to grow in our lives, so that it vibrates out from us into the intelligent, benevolent, and responsive Zero Point Field. The truth is that God gives us what we want and what we ask for, and we demonstrate what we want— and ask for it—through our *attention*, not just our intention. Our attention is a constant vibration that ripples out to this responsive energy field around us and, through this energy soup of connectedness, we become readily joined to all other things that are vibrating at a matching frequency.

When our attention, and consequently our prayer request, is rooted in desperation and pleading, we send out a vibration of powerlessness. When our attention is filled with wishing for what we don't have, we send out a message of scarcity. When we're focused on our complaints, we increase what's wrong. When we wallow in resentment and self-pity, we create more isolation and lack of love. When we dwell on our worries, we feed our fears. As we give our attention this way, we demonstrate that we are choosing pain over peace. When we're attached to being right about everything that's wrong, we demonstrate we value our certainty and self-righteousness more than happiness. Is it any wonder that God fulfills our requests by giving us more of the same?

If our requests don't get answered in the way we hoped, we probably need to change the way we're asking. A 180-degree turnaround may be in order to turn a "pleading" request into a "giving" one. This means replacing disempowered wishing with gratitude by giving thanks for unanswered prayers as though they've already been fulfilled. We can turn complaining around by focusing on what we can do in a situation instead of what's wrong with it. We can change resentment into forgiveness. If it's hard to forgive, start with yourself. If it's still difficult, ask yourself this question frequently: would you rather have God answer your prayers by proving you right or by making you happy? When we find our mind crowded with worries, this is the time for faith. We can always reach up to a Higher Power. Recognize that personal power may not be enough to get us through, but Higher Power is. You can start the process of turning your prayer requests around by simply becoming more aware of your thoughts.

Who or What Is God?

Our next experiment is a group prayer on behalf of ourselves, for the people we love, and for the world.* Prayer is as varied as every individual who prays, and there are a multitude of approaches to it, as well as definitions of what it is. We will work with prayer as a channel of communication between our consciousness and something greater that we call God. Before we enter into our experiment, perhaps some attention needs to be given to the word *God*. I know many devoutly spiritual people who take offense at the very word because it's so tied in with religious dogma that doesn't fit their spiritual framework.

---

*Just a quick word on the ethics of praying for others and whether we need permission to pray for another person: I hold that as long as we're praying for the highest good, it's not necessary to ask permission or tell the recipient that we're praying on his or her behalf. The minute we start praying for a specific outcome, as in "I'll pray that you have a full recovery from your illness," we need permission. Specific outcomes are our human agendas, not necessarily God's.

Others embrace God, yet have rigid and narrow definitions of what God is. In all the ways the word *God* is used, can it ever be more than a hopelessly inadequate shorthand for something too big to capture in words? In chapter 8, I drew some correlation between God and the Zero Point Field, suggesting the Field may well be at the heart of what world religions have all struggled to grasp and define in their very different ways.

If you have a well-constructed concept of God and spirituality, whether it comes from what you've been taught, a reaction against what you've been taught, or what you've come to on your own, consider letting it go, if only briefly, to give yourself an opportunity to have a bigger experience of God. Recall the chapter 5 exercise, "Let Go of What You Think You Know" and apply it to all you thought you knew for sure about God:

> *Imagine all you thought you knew for certain is not true. Don't assume this means the opposite is true or what you most fear is true. You don't need to figure out what is true or to understand the how and why of this. Simply play with it as an exercise in imagination. As you release your current interpretations, don't immediately grasp for new ones. Simply let your mind open, and allow yourself to be confused. This process is much like letting your eyes go out of focus so you're seeing the color, form, and the big picture of the world around you rather than the details. Imagine that even in the midst of confusion and not knowing, you're safe and at peace.*

The Power of Group Prayer

The first time I led a group in the following prayer was in a seminar I was teaching in Florida. Shortly afterward, I received a phone message from my husband at home in Minneapolis telling me not to worry if I heard news reports of tornadoes touching down in our city. Apparently, at the same time we were praying for the well-being of our personal and collective communities, a series of tornadoes touched down all around my home. One hit the parking lot where my husband's car was parked, but no damage was done to his vehicle. One touched down around the corner from my house, but missed us entirely. Others touched down all around my rental property, downing a neighbor's tree and blowing huge debris into my yard, but not damaging my building. What's more, in spite of devastating property damage that wrecked whole blocks and even downed the huge steeple of a church in a heavily populated urban area, no deaths and few injuries were reported. The disaster brought people out into the streets to help each other, many meeting neighbors for the first time. Miracle or coincidence? Try it for yourself and then decide.

Before reading further, take a moment to identify your own personal intention you'd like to take into prayer. This could be a request for healing, for guidance, for resolving an issue in your life, or anything for which you'd like Divine assistance. Your intention may also include other people for whom you'd like to pray. Again, for best results, wait until you have some uninterrupted time for this so that you can go into a quiet, meditative state.

Experiment
Praying for Ourselves and Others

Relax your body, and quiet your thoughts with some deep, slow breaths. Once again, let your sense of identification shift from "particle" reality to "wave" reality. Feel your physical body becoming soft, relaxed, and weightless. 🦋 🦋 🦋 Feel the particles that make up your physical body begin to gently vibrate and spread apart, leaving more and more space in between. God fills the space in between. Soon, even those wide-spaced particles melt into the Light of God, and what was once dense matter is now a beautiful wave of light energy, free of all the laws that limit matter. Take a moment to simply be in the energy of God, recognizing that God is everywhere; there is no place God isn't. 🦋 🦋 🦋

Now see the network of other readers, past, present, and future, with you, all vibrating together in the Light and Love of God. Together we amplify the energy of God exponentially. Anything becomes possible. Through our joined consciousness, what has seemed difficult in the past is now becoming easy. Take a moment to feel the God energy of the network building. 🦋 🦋 🦋

Imagine us all surrounded and immersed in the presence of God. You may see angelic figures, beings of light, and specific religious figures, or envision this in a more abstract way simply as the Light of Divine Love and Higher Mind. Imagine this presence to be wholly benevolent, devoid of any judgment or punishment, and highly responsive to our desires for assistance. Although we aren't always open to it, this spiritual presence is always with us, guiding us, loving us, and taking great joy in our many experiences of earthly life. It doesn't see us in terms of successes and failures. Instead It sees us deepening through our experience, becoming richer and more complex as souls.

Surrounded by the perfect peace of this loving presence, bring your prayer intention gently to mind. Hold it lightly in your thoughts—like you would a butterfly. Look deeply into your request to discern what's at the heart of it. What are you truly calling out for? Is it joy, freedom, healing, ease, love, security, inspiration, forgiveness, peace, creativity, or something else entirely? 🦋 🦋 🦋

Find a bit of the joy and wholeness you want already living inside you, and grow it bigger so you fill yourself with the inner feeling of having your request already fulfilled. Becoming the fulfillment you desire—that is how God hears your request. Let the inner experience of having all that you need and want flow into gratitude and ripple outward as a gift back to Spirit.

The vibration of gratitude creates the inner state of willingness and availability to healing. It gives God an open door and "permission" to speed up your transformation. So take a moment to let your burdens and worries be lifted from your shoulders. Hand them all over, and let your heart simply feel light and overflowing with love. Know the benevolent presence of God is working with you on many levels, mostly outside your awareness, to assist your growth. To become as conscious of this process as you can, let your body relax completely, your mind becoming soft and open, and ask to hear, feel, or be shown whatever you most need to know at this time for your highest good. ❦ ❦ ❦ When this feels complete, let go of your own request. Let it fly away.

Now we will offer prayer on behalf of others. Begin by bringing to mind our network of readers. Then bring to mind any individuals in your life whom you would like to hold in prayer, unconditionally, for their highest good. And finally, hold in mind the entire world, letting your mind touch lightly upon areas and issues in need of healing. Hold these "issues" lightly in peace, not darkly in despair. Now with all these groups and individuals softly in mind, say the following healing decree. It doesn't matter if you say it silently or out loud. It is important that you say it with power.

A Healing Decree

Let our hearts and minds now unite with all others
in service to Divine Will, making us
an unstoppable force as we decree:

By the Grace of God, Divine Love and Guidance
now flow to all those in this network
who have prayed for help!

By the Grace of God, Divine Love and Guidance
now flow to every member of our
personal communities!

By the Grace of God, Divine Love and Guidance
now flow to the Earth and All of Creation!

- Thank you, Divine Spirit.
I have faith in the reality of Miracles.
I know the power of Love.
I surrender to Divine Will.
Let the Divine Design now manifest!

Bring your prayer and meditation time to a close by sending thanks to the others in our network of readers and to the angelic beings and spiritual helpers who have assisted us. End with some deep full breaths. As you come back to an awareness of your physical body, feel every cell refreshed with vitality and health, the density of matter now infused with the life force of God.

18

It Didn't Work!

AVING SPENT MUCH OF MY CAREER challenging groups to manifest miracles in a variety of contexts, including in-person healings, online study programs, group phone conferences, and now here, through the words on these pages, I've found that a challenge extended as a collaborative experiment, presented with excitement and faith, never fails to elicit miracles. As I write this, I have no doubt whatsoever that as soon as these words find readers, the miracle stories will start pouring in. I also know others will write to me in disappointment, telling me it didn't work. Some will be sad, some angry. All will be a bit stubborn in their certainty that "It didn't work!"

As satisfying as it is to be right, clinging to certainty can trap us in our own limitations. One of my favorite illustrations of this is a story Price Pritcett tells at the beginning of his book on personal effectiveness, titled *you2*. He describes watching a housefly bashing itself to death trying to get outside through a screen window. All of its limited housefly senses told it that straight ahead was the way out. It could see it, smell it, practically taste it, yet the more it tried, the more beaten and battered it became. If only the fly could have seen the bigger picture, it would have been able to turn around in the opposite direction and fly easily through an open door.

ow we often operate in life. We become fixated on the
route that is most obvious to our physical senses, and we
ne it's not only the best but the only route to our goal. Then
we imit our possibilities and wind up pursuing a path that not
only won't take us where we want to go, but may even destroy
us in the process. If you are feeling doubtful that miracles will
ever find you, this exercise is especially for you.

Exercise

Make Your Best Case

Make your best case for why it didn't work, won't work, never
works for you. Spend the day defending your story to yourself.
Convince yourself that you're right. Put it in writing if you like.
Notice how much emotional energy is invested in your story.
If making your case is easy to do, if it keeps coming to mind
during the day, or if the whole exercise just makes you angry,
then you can be fairly certain that you still have a lot invested
in this story being right.

At the end of the day, decide whether you'd rather be right about
your story or receive miracles, blessings, and Grace. If you'd
rather be right, put this book down, and don't pick it up again. If,
on the other hand, you feel a little like a bashed-up fly, ready to
try a new direction, even if it makes no sense at all, proceed to
the next chapter and exercise.

19
Cultivating a Miracle Mind

IF YOU IMAGINE EACH THOUGHT going through your mind as a seed destined to grow the events of your future, how do you feel about the quality of the seeds you're planting? Are they growing success, joy, and love, or bitterness, pain, and disappointment? Where does your attention go when you're not actively engaged in some specific mental focus—when you're alone driving in your car, taking a break from work, or cooking dinner? Do you tend to dwell more on everything wrong in your life: resentments, past hurts, future worries? Or do you fill your thoughts with what you love: happy successes, love that you've shared, gratitude in the present, and pleasant anticipation of the future?

Most of us have certain patterns of thought that are so habitual we're not even fully aware of them. These thoughts that pop into mind when we're not focused on anything in particular reflect learned habits, probably acquired when we were very young. We may have habits of worry or optimism, of faith or bitterness. The areas of our lives that flow easily reflect our positive automatic thoughts. On the other hand, we may tell ourselves many times a day life is unfair, we're unsafe, or we don't deserve to be happy. We may be so unaware of this inner conversation that we don't even call these messages thoughts; we call them reality, and we unconsciously attract life circumstances that match them.

Monitoring every random thought can be a daunting task. However, a much more doable exercise that can powerfully affect thinking is to simply monitor what we say out loud. So the next exercise is one of giving up whining.

The first time I did this exercise myself, I made a three-month commitment to it, which only lasted fifteen minutes before I almost broke my commitment and "whined." I caught myself just in the nick of time, but it made me instantly aware of how automatic complaining can be.

Interestingly, once I got the hang of not whining, I found my inner dialogue changing along with my spoken words. It just wasn't as satisfying to whine to myself anymore. After practicing this for several weeks, I noticed that any number of things I usually struggled with were falling into place with miraculous ease.

It also forced me to find a different way of sharing with my friends that wasn't based on commiserating. I didn't suddenly become an always-smiling Pollyanna but, when I did share what was painful in my life, I did it in a way that left me feeling more empowered afterward. I reached out for help, not just sympathy. What's more, some of my friends later reported that their words and thoughts underwent a change, too. They stopped whining to me in response to my not whining to them. This enhanced the quality of our relating and had an effect on my friends that they took with them beyond our interaction.

Exercise
Give Up Whining!

Starting now and continuing for one month, let go of all talk and all conversations in which you present yourself as an unfortunate victim of circumstances beyond your control. If you slip and catch yourself in a whine, redirect it by acknowledging your own participation in bringing this situation about. Share what you're willing to do to change your experience. Or share what hidden lessons or blessings you're receiving from this experience. Perhaps ask the person with whom you're speaking for help. The help might be for changing your situation or just your state of mind. In other words, it's okay to feel bad and talk about it. When you do, however, speak as though it's an experience you had something to do with bringing about, have the power to change, and are learning something from. Even if you don't fully believe this, speaking as though you have power in your situation will help it to be so. The less you think and speak as a victim, the less you will be one.

To up the effectiveness of this exercise, do it for one month in an absolute way as a symbolic act, which means you will give it added power by giving it a bigger significance. Tell yourself that if you are willing to absolutely eliminate victim speech, you can manifest whatever highest good you most desire. Assume this really is true so that when you're tempted to cheat, your question to yourself becomes, "If my most heartfelt dreams coming to fruition depend upon me choosing not to complain about my life right now, what do I choose? What do I love more, complaining or having my heart's desires?"

The total, absolute, never-cheating-even-once aspect of this assignment is important because it strengthens your focus and will, making whatever you set your mind to easier to accomplish. So the rule of this game is if you slip you need to start over again, recommitting for a new one-month period. Or if you don't want to begin again, you can go back to the person you complained to and admit that you didn't mean what you said. Then revise your story away from disempowered whining. If you want to make it through a month without whining and just can't seem to do it, consider there may be a payoff for you in remaining in a victim role. This will become clearer in the next chapters.

20

Mastery and Self-Responsibility

TRULY, DAZZLING DISPLAYS OF MANIFESTATION are easy. I've seen people create amazing results, often immediately: jobs and opportunities opening up; important new relationships beginning; old relationships healing; houses, cars, and all sorts of material things appearing according to the receivers' wishes; lump sums of money showing up unexpectedly; incomes increasing; symptoms of illness disappearing; even cavities in teeth spontaneously healing. So please expect no less for yourself.

However, I've also seen people create an astonishing result—for example, someone needing money, praying for it, and almost instantaneously having a large check show up from an entirely unexpected source—yet barely acknowledging the blessing of it. These folks may have success using manifesting techniques but without seeing much change in their overall quality of life. Creating results doesn't ensure that we'll find happiness in those results, find peace of mind, or be able to produce similar results in every area of life, like those circumstances that remain painfully stuck no matter what we do.

If we want to experience the kind of mastery that enhances quality of life, we need to look, not just at our power to manifest occasional, lovely coincidences, but also at our responsibility for the unlovely coincidences of life that we call "circumstances beyond our control." Our power to affect the world around us through our conscious intent expands in direct correlation with our willingness to recognize the connection between our inner state and outer reality, barring nothing, the pleasant and the unpleasant.

While many will accept this concept of self-responsibility to a point, the notion of absolute self-responsibility tends to be unpopular, and choosing not to accept it doesn't mean we'll never experience success or happiness. It simply means we won't have as much access to the magical coincidences that cut corners and make life easier. So this principle is for those who are very serious about making a "quantum leap," as opposed to simply making progress, and there's no right or wrong choice around this. We all have a pace and a path that's right for us.

When I speak on the principle of self-responsibility to groups, the argument invariably comes up that there will *always* be things that we can't control, that we can't help, that have nothing to do with us. Many offer examples of things that, from the Newtonian paradigm of separateness and randomness, certainly appear out of anyone's control to affect. However, if we shift into the quantum model of connectedness, how can any piece of the whole not affect all of the whole?

It's not that the argument against absolute self-responsibility is wrong. It's that, as physics is demonstrating, seemingly mutually exclusive realities can both be true. The phenomenon of two seemingly incompatible realities coexisting has a name: the Principle of Complementarity. The Principle was first formulated by physicist Niels Bohr, an early pioneer of atomic physics. Fred Alan Wolf writes about this phenomenon in his book, *Taking the Quantum Leap,* saying Complementarity "taught us that our everyday senses were not to be trusted to give a total view of reality. There was always a hidden, complementary side to everything we experienced." Furthermore, he writes, "The more we determine one side of reality, the less the other, equally true side is shown to us." In other words, the more we focus on one perspective of reality and hold it to be the only truth, the less we're able to see other perspectives. This is why flexible thinking and unlearning everything we think we know for certain is such a crucial ingredient in miracle-making.

Miracles happen in natural accordance with spiritual law. If we want miracle-making principles to work for us consistently, we need to be willing to work with them as absolutes. If we hold that we sometimes have the power to determine our reality but not always, where, then, do we draw the line? How do we decide when spiritual law is in effect and when it's not? Ultimately, the more we hold that we only sometimes have the power to be miracle-makers, the more we'll live a life filled with unpleasant circumstances outside our control.

The resistance that comes up around this principle is understandable. Absolute self-responsibility is an idea the ego can so easily run away with, and then, when things go well, we become obnoxiously full of ourselves. We feel a little better than everyone else, a little more evolved. Taken to extreme, this becomes delusional "magical thinking" and a sign of deteriorating mental health. The flip side of this coin is that when things don't go according to our wishes, we beat ourselves up and resolve to become better control freaks dedicated to eating right, thinking right, talking right, breathing right, and more, believing that if we control our every waking act we'll never again have an unpleasant experience.

The ego, as I'm using the term, is the part of us that believes we are defined by the limits of our physical body and, thus, are vulnerable and separate. The ego looks at the world through a filter of judgment in which everything is either better than or lesser than everything else. It is "particle" consciousness rather than "wave" consciousness.

When the ego embraces this principle of self-responsibility, it becomes abusive and much abused. Consequently, it's crucial to understand and head off the pitfalls of this very powerful principle, or it will be more detrimental than helpful.

Blame, Shame, and Self-Responsibility

Before the principle of self-responsibility can be useful, it has to be unraveled from the whole paradigm of blame and shame. The more we bristle at the idea of self-responsibility, the more likely it is that we were taught at an early age to feel shame. Blame and shame go hand in hand, one giving rise to the other. They both have to do with finding fault, pointing a finger of judgment, and defining something or someone as "wrong." For those of us who've been taught to feel shame, it's unbearable to let go of blame because then, all the energy that had been going into blaming external forces for what's wrong has nowhere to go except toward ourselves. Then we swing from feeling victimized by external circumstances to shaming and victimizing ourselves. While the experience of being an out-of-control victim is certainly not pleasant, at least it allows us to feel innocent rather than shamed and to feel justified in being angry at our circumstances.

Self-responsibility can be a crushing burden when carried this way. For example, many have applied the idea of self-responsibility to physical illness in a way that assumes an ill person has done something terribly wrong to create his or her disease. Others hold a perspective that they are somehow less spiritually evolved if the outer circumstances of their lives don't reflect joy, abundance, and health all the time.

The catch in this way of thinking is that our conscious control only affects those aspects of self that are within the range of conscious awareness. Painful and unexpected challenges are often the catalysts that heighten our awareness of limiting beliefs and patterns that have been operating at an unconscious level. Most of us have an assortment of conscious and unconscious, sometimes conflicting, agendas operating to create our experience in life. An example of conflicting agendas would be a person who very much wants to heal from an illness, yet receives so much benefit from the rest and caring attention resulting from the illness, that an unconscious investment is made in maintaining whatever circumstances are needed (such as the illness) to keep these rewards coming. Another example would be a person who longs to be in a relationship, yet unconsciously fears that an intimate partnership would mean the loss of personal freedom or would lead to painful abandonment.

When these secondary, but powerful, agendas are present, we often have the experience of spinning wheels. Even though we direct a lot of effort toward our conscious desire, we don't seem to make any progress. And we won't make progress—until the less conscious agenda is somehow addressed or released. It's often through the challenging experiences in life that we have an opportunity to recognize and change these hidden agendas so we can stop being at cross purposes with ourselves.

Blame and shame are disempowering, often immobilizing, emotions that keep us unconscious and don't motivate us to be better people. They need to be tossed out altogether for the work we're doing here. Shifting from blame and shame to self-responsibility means looking at what you don't like about your life, not as something you did wrong (shame), or as something done to you by circumstances beyond your control (blame), but with the question, "How does this situation show what I've learned to expect from life?"

Take, for example, the experience of being a victim of violent crime or abuse of any sort: the distortion of self-responsibility would be to assume, "I must have done something to deserve or ask for this." The more positive application is to examine how you've been trained to expect danger or abuse as part of life. How have your previous life experiences taught you that you're not safe? The opportunity here is to learn compassion for yourself, experience forgiveness for another, and begin to develop a deeper understanding of your own safety that will ultimately keep you safer physically. As a counselor many years ago, I noticed that my women clients who had been raped had almost all been subjected to sexual or physical abuse as children. They learned early in life to expect to be harmed. No one had ever taught them that they had a right to be safe. These painful beliefs about life can even be evolved in very productive ways: we can learn to protect ourselves, we can advocate for victims, we can fight victimizers, and we can develop our strength. These are all very useful and helpful things. They simply aren't the same as learning to be safe.

Finding the Hidden Gains

Self-responsibility means asking yourself what value a painful situation might hold and how it serves you. If you look closely enough, there's invariably a gain. For instance, sometimes we fill up our lives with energy-draining obstacles because on some level we're not ready for what we think we'd rather be doing. If we never have time or opportunity to pursue our dreams, we never have an opportunity to fail. Or if we're constantly a victim of circumstances beyond our control, we can ask for people's support and empathy and have less expected of us than if we had not fallen upon "hard luck." There are hidden gains in even the most unpleasant life experiences.

Once, for example, I was driving to an appointment feeling irritated and rushed. I had promised myself a week earlier to break a habit of angry thinking in which I played over in my mind all my annoyances until I felt truly awful. On this particular day, I'd lapsed into old habits, and my mind was wallowing in crankiness. Suddenly, a car in front of me slammed on the brakes, and I was just able to screech to a stop without hitting it. The car behind me, however, kept right on going into my bumper. The collision wasn't my fault, and in my state of irritation I could have felt victimized and called it one more annoying event in an already bad day. Instead, I let it jolt me out of anger. Afterward, it occurred to me that the minor accident was a perfect reflection of the state my mind was in when it happened. It even seemed to be an answer to my prayer for help in releasing angry thoughts. There was no serious damage done, I was only slightly bumped, and it completely knocked all the angry thoughts out of my head. As I drove the rest of the distance to my appointment I felt at peace for the first time that day.

The power in self-responsibility is that once we start seeing our own contributions to our circumstances, we can change them. If the world is treating you badly, look to see how this could be a reflection of how you treat yourself. Are you self-critical? Do you put everyone else's needs before your own? Do you get so caught up in doing what's expected of you, and what you think you should do, that you have no time left to explore what you want to do? These are just a few ways we may manifest our lack of self-love and acceptance.

Another frequent argument made against self-responsibility is that God creates our reality—we don't. The essence of self-responsibility is neither about putting our will before God's or putting God's will above our own. Ultimately, it's a call to heal our perceived separateness from God so there is only One Will. This, of course, means quieting the fears and grandiosity of our ego's voice. No small task, but definitely worth the effort.

Questions for Thought

If all the circumstances of your life—the ones you love and the ones you don't—reflect exactly what you've learned to expect from life (not necessarily what you want or consciously ask for, just what you've learned through experience to expect), what would this tell you about your expectations? Which expectations would you like to change?

Exercise
No Circumstances Beyond Our Control

Today, say over and over as many times as you can manage, "There are no circumstances beyond my control."* Say this

---

*Many people versed in affirmation practices balk at this affirmation that "breaks the rules" of affirmations with its negative phrasing, and they want to reword it. For best results, I suggest you leave it as it. It's deliberately phrased to start you imagining all the circumstances that seem impossibly out of your control so that your mind can then confirm, "Yup, not even that!"

silently to yourself. Say it out loud. Write it down and post it where you'll see it. Put yourself to sleep tonight saying this repeatedly. It doesn't matter if you don't believe it. Say it as though you believe it. Imagine how it would feel if you did believe it. After giving your full attention to this exercise for a day, continue it for as long as you like as you move on to the next chapters' exercises.

21
Finding the Gift

WHEN WE MOVE BEYOND BLAME AND SHAME, we're able to experience challenging life situations from a place of acceptance rather than judgment. Far from being an attitude of weakness, it's through acceptance that we unlock surprising powers and resources to transform our situation.

I once knew a woman who lived with melanoma for many years. This extremely dangerous form of skin cancer required her to have painful surgeries every six weeks to remove precancerous growths. She struggled through periods of anger, fear, and depression over her illness, and related to the cancer as an enemy to be combated. Finally, after reading one of Catherine Ponder's many classic books on spiritual healing, she decided to make friends with her body and her disease. Every day she wrote pages of the affirmation "Thank you, God, for cancer." At first the words felt untrue and hard to write, but she kept at it week after week. Gradually she stopped feeling like a victim of her illness, and soon her six-week check-ups were detecting no precancerous tissue. More than a year later she was still clear of cancerous growth.

We always have a choice around how to interpret the life circumstances we've experienced in the past or present. The most harshest or most tragic events may be the greatest turning points of our lives. That doesn't mean we need to call pain to us in order to grow. I believe growth happens in the release of pain rather than through the experience of it. As we let go of our perception of ourselves as victims, we take a big step toward releasing pain from our lives.

Many of us feel victimized by our past and "damaged" as a result. Yet perhaps on some level we've called these extreme experiences into our lives to help us tap into our greatness and transcend the belief in our vulnerability. I grew up with a cruel, abusive father who went out of his way to shame and torment me. On one hand, I can blame him for any number of wounds and challenges I've had to overcome. On the other hand, I don't think I'd be doing the work I'm doing today, or have the strengths, values, joys, and love I have in my life now, if it weren't for the experiences I had with my father. As we stop calling our circumstances "bad" and our experiences "painful," they lose their charge to hurt and control us. As we stop defining ourselves as victims, we stop being victims.

Ultimately, any situation that persists in spite of our not wanting it has some hidden value. It may be meeting a need, helping us grow, or keeping us safe. The following exercise includes a number of questions to help bring these hidden payoffs to light. The payoffs to painful circumstances are often difficult to see, and many people's first response is a hot defense that they are certainly not gaining from them! Yet with a little help, even the loudest protesters typically find something. Perhaps their illness allows them to ask for things they never would request if they were well, or maybe a lack of income provides protection from other people's needs and expectations. Maybe a cluttered house keeps unwanted company away, or a relationship falls apart because it's not really serving either partner's growth any more. If you can see no possible gains to a challenging situation in your life, I encourage you to keep asking and looking deeper until you do.

These unconscious agendas sometimes come from undeveloped, childlike parts of ourselves that protect us by using coping strategies we learned in childhood and thus keep us locked in old behavior. For example, if we received a lot of rewards for being sick when we were young, later in life when we need rewards, we're likely to get sick in order to feel deserving of them. We can break this cycle by giving ourselves the special attention we crave separate from the experience of illness.

Other equally unconscious agendas come from a higher, God-powered place that calls crises into our lives when we're resisting growth. Then life circumstances evict us from our comfort zone and push us toward our higher good, ready or not. Think of the story in chapter 14 of the man who asked for a better relationship with "Kathy" and had to go through a painful end to his marriage to find a better relationship with someone new (also named Kathy). We can break the cycle of crisis by learning to move with change, embracing it willingly before it becomes a devastating breakdown.

Some of our life circumstances, I believe, come from a soul level where we choose, not for the purpose of ease, but for enrichment. For example, I knew a very wise and loving woman who was born with a degenerative disease that took her life when she was still in her early thirties. She believed very strongly there was an important spiritual purpose to her physical disability, that her life lesson was to love life in spite of any pain and limitation her body created. A believer in reincarnation, she felt certain that she had committed suicide in a previous life and had "chosen" her current situation to help her learn to love life no matter what. By the end of her life, she unquestionably did, in spite of severe pain and disablement. We can let go of feeling victimized, even by most extreme circumstances, by finding the gift in our challenges and being grateful.

Exercise
Receiving the Gain Without the Pain

STEP ONE

Start by identifying a challenging situation in your life, one in which you feel at the mercy of circumstances beyond your control. It could be anything, such as a health condition, a recurring relationship pattern, or any situation in which you feel stuck and no amount of effort seems to have an impact.

STEP TWO

Next, ask yourself how this condition is serving you. What is it helping you, allowing you, or forcing you to do, be, or have that you wouldn't otherwise experience? Identify even the things that you wouldn't define as positive.

1. Is it forcing you to let others help you?

2. Is it causing you to spend your time differently? If so, what might be the gain in this?

3. Are you receiving attention (positive or negative) that you wouldn't otherwise get? If so, how is this attention giving you something you need or expect? (Sometimes negative attention preserves a familiar identity we're not ready to let go of or keeps people from expecting too much from us, to name just a couple of possible gains.)

4. Are you developing strengths and resources that you wouldn't have without this situation?

5. Is the situation preserving a familiar identity? If so, what is that identity? What might you lose that you don't want to lose if you acted outside your own box?

6. Is it allowing you to put off doing something burdensome or frightening?

7. Is the condition protecting you from failing by preventing you from beginning something?

8. Does it distract you and keep your attention away from things that are too painful to look at? (Sometimes the challenging issue we can never seem to resolve is there because, if it were gone, we'd have to deal with things far more painful. For example, money or health crises may take all our attention so we never have time or energy to look at intimacy challenges.)

9. Does it allow you to avoid painful or frightening emotions, such as anger, sadness, guilt, or shame?

10. Does it give you permission to say "No," to get angry, to be selfish, to grieve?

11. Are your relationships with others affected by this condition? Have they deepened as a result? Does the condition create "space" interpersonally: fewer relationships, more privacy, or more time alone? Does this condition offer protection from intimacy and possible hurts that could result from getting close?

STEP THREE

What would you need to do to receive the gains of this situation without needing the pain? The true answer to this question invariably involves some form of risk and stretching beyond your comfort zone. Keep exploring this question until you find where the risk is for you. This will be where the greatest healing lies.

For example, I did this exercise with a woman who had breast cancer. For her, the secondary gains of her illness involved putting herself first for once. As an assignment, I suggested she invite a group of her friends to form a healing committee for her. This committee would support her recovery in many different ways, including practical assistance, prayer, and emotional support. I suggested she make and distribute a wish list with a large variety of specific ways in which her friends could help her. The woman was comfortable with all of these suggestions until I added that she ask her friends if they would be willing to continue supporting her in this way even after she released her illness. She could justify deserving so much attention when she was fighting for her life, but she had difficulty feeling worthy of it without the illness. This last step was where the biggest risk lay—and also the biggest healing.

To truly be ready to release a challenging condition, we need to willingly build into our lives whatever the condition has been forcing us to be or do, without waiting for life circumstances to give us no choice. Generally, these steps require that we act outside of our long-held conditioning, going against what we've been taught we "should" do to become more authentically who we are. It might mean speaking your truth even when it doesn't fit with your conditioning to be nice, or taking a "well day" off from work when you need a break instead of waiting for the flu to knock you out for a week. If you prefer doing things for yourself, you may need to cultivate habits of reaching out to others and accepting help. If you're always the strong one, you may need to learn how to share control and show vulnerability without a crisis forcing you to.

See if you can think of several things you could to do to give yourself the gains without the pain of your situation. Some, if not all, of these are bound to feel like a big step out of your comfort zone. If not, you probably haven't correctly identified the true payoffs for you. You don't have to be willing to do the things you come up with at this time. Simply identifying them is a powerful first step that will start change in motion. Action will follow when you're ready to live without the gains of your condition.

STEP FOUR

If you feel completely unable to identify the hidden gains of a completely stuck area of your life, know that the gains are probably important enough that you're not ready to see them, let alone release them. And that's not a bad thing. Remember, this isn't about shame or blame. There may be things you're learning from a painful situation that aren't meant to be rushed through, and it may serve you more to practice acceptance. You might follow the example of my friend with melanoma and work with your own affirmation of gratitude: "Thank you, God, for this experience in my life." Keep working with this affirmation every day until you feel the truth of what you're writing and a sense of peace around the situation. Or turn it over in prayer, and ask to be shown a way to receive the lessons or gains of this situation differently without pain and struggle.

22
Paradigm Shifts

WHAT WOULD YOU GIVE TO MAKE SOMETHING you've struggled with, something that seems impossibly difficult, suddenly become astonishingly easy? Can you imagine what it would feel like to have a painfully stuck area of your life shift so that the path clears, hard work is no longer needed, and what you've been wanting (or something so much better that it makes what you wanted pale in comparison) is not only within reach, but in hand? This isn't as impossible as it seems. If you're already thinking, "This is one of those things that happens to other people, not to me," realize you've already had this experience over and over again: when you learned to walk, talk, ride a bike, drive a car, and probably any number of occasions that you called "good luck." It just hasn't happened yet in your current area of struggle.

Creating this shift from struggle to ease is sometimes achieved through the perseverance of learning a new skill, as in some of the examples I mentioned. Other times it can be accomplished nearly instantaneously with an inner shift that allows radically new circumstances to fall into place. One woman, for example, attended my five-day intensive workshop wanting to resolve her ongoing struggle with finding satisfying employment. She went through a lot of personal transformation during the five days and ended the workshop with renewed optimism and excitement about resuming her job search. But she never got that far. Right before the last session of the workshop, someone arrived who wasn't part of our group. She was lost and stumbled into our church basement accidentally, looking for a meeting being held in another church. As it turned out, the woman in my workshop knew her—had sought employment from her, in fact. It had been just the kind of work she wanted, but unfortunately there were no positions available. The two women greeted each other and shared a moment of conversation. As she was leaving, the second woman said, "By the way, are you still interested in a job? I have a position open, and you'd be perfect! Call me tomorrow if you're interested." This serendipitous meeting did result in a very fulfilling job situation, and she had done nothing to make it happen other than change herself inwardly.

Still another way to transform struggle is through a change in perspective or attitude, which allows us to see options that didn't seem to be there before, or to simply find peace in a situation that was once intolerable. For example, once when I was in the midst of leading a six-month-long training program, I wound up leaving my job with the sponsoring organization only three months into the program. There was no one to take my place leading this group, yet I dreaded the thought of three more months of work for a job I had left. I had emphasized to participants the importance of making a commitment to attend the full six months, so I felt my integrity was on the line. I felt obligated to keep my commitment, but was doing so grudgingly. After a week or two of this, it suddenly occurred to me that there could be another option besides deserting my group or miserably carrying on with the class. I decided to make the next three months the best group experience of my life. I had no particular plan for how to do this; I just held the idea in my mind. Very quickly the group reflected my intention back to me by becoming more bonded, open, and willing to take risks. It did, in fact, evolve into the most powerful and fulfilling group experience I'd ever had. By the end, I looked forward to those classes as a high point of my week and wouldn't have missed them for the world.

These examples describe changes that I think of as paradigm shifts. It's hard to explain how to have a paradigm shift, and when we're in the midst of struggle, this miraculous transformation can seem impossibly elusive. Yet once we've had one, we wonder why we never saw things so simply before. Think of the housefly described in chapter 18 that was battering itself silly trying to get out of a screen window, even in the presence of an open door just a short flight in the opposite direction. Increasing effort wasn't effective. A new approach was required. Flexibility, openness, and vision—not necessarily hard work—lead to a paradigm shift. It requires letting go of certainty and stubbornness so we can choose how we want to experience life.

The following exercise will help you transform some area of struggle in your life. Although there's no sure linear route to a paradigm shift, here's a linear process that can sometimes successfully "trick" our housefly mind into seeing differently. You may be surprised to find you already have all the resources you need to create ease. For this exercise, it's particularly important that you complete each step before you read ahead to the next.

Exercise
Turn Struggle to Ease

STEP ONE

Identify an area of your life where you currently experience struggle and want to create ease. If there are many such areas, choose just one, picking the one that has the greatest emotional charge.

STEP TWO

Give some attention to the payoffs remaining stuck may have for you. As we covered in-depth in the last chapters, any condition that causes us misery, yet persists, is serving us in some way. If not for the payoff, we would have found a way to change. Payoffs aren't necessarily obvious or easy to spot. Sometimes we unconsciously fill our lives with energy-draining obstacles, because on some level we're not ready for the responsibility, the risks, or the change that would come with what we think we want. Perhaps being in the role of victim allows us to receive help, attention, and love that we wouldn't get otherwise. Sometimes a painful condition is forcing us to choose more healthful priorities or develop strengths. It might preserve a familiar identity or lifestyle so we don't have to stretch and grow. As you identify the payoffs in your own situation, give some thought to whether you're willing to live without them. As long as we need the payoffs of a painful condition, we will unconsciously hold it in place.

STEP THREE

Next, give some thought to how you would feel if the outcome you most want were offered to you right now without any steps, struggle, or time invested. Would it feel overwhelming? Would you feel deserving? Would it still feel as precious to you, or does the reward feel diminished somehow without the effort? Sometimes we have such an ingrained belief that anything worth having requires hard work ("No pain, no gain") that we automatically believe anything we haven't worked for isn't valuable. Simply identifying this kind of thinking will begin to diffuse its power to limit our options.

STEP FOUR

Now take a moment to become still and relaxed. 🦋 🦋 🦋 Take a few deep breaths and let your attention turn inward. Take a moment to feel the presence of God energy within and around you. Invite the limitless wisdom of God to guide and assist you in this exercise. 🦋 🦋 🦋

Allow to come to mind a time from your past when something that had once been an incredible struggle became remarkably easy. Don't think too hard about this; just see what pops into mind first. It could be an incident from your recent past or your early childhood or anywhere in between. Ease might have come from effort or luck or any number of ways. Again, just let an experience pop into mind, and see what comes first. Don't go on to the next step until a past experience is clearly in mind.

STEP FIVE

Trust that your higher wisdom put this particular experience into your mind rather than any others that could have come to you, because it holds some keys for how to resolve your current situation. Imagine that in some way what you did then can be applied to your situation now. So ask yourself, "What did I do in this previous situation that changed it?" Did you develop a new skill? Did you let other people help you? Did you open to an option you had been stubbornly resisting? Did you just relax and let yourself forget the struggle for a while, so when you looked at it again, it easily resolved? Did you act out of character, speak your truth, or do something you don't usually do? Imagine that whatever you did then has some bearing on what you need to do now. See how this might guide you to a specific action or a change in attitude.

STEP SIX

Finally, take a moment to recall the inner experience of ease after struggle that you had in this past experience. Bring it so clearly to mind that the feelings of success, relief, empowerment, and effortlessness you had then seem vividly real in your imagination now. Imagine feeling this same way in your current situation. See yourself having already resolved any difficulty and looking back on your time of struggle as though it has already faded into the past. You don't need to see the steps, actions, or outcomes that led you from struggle to ease. Simply immerse yourself in the inner feeling that things have already shifted.

STEP SEVEN

Now let go of trying to have a paradigm shift. Instead, reflect on the times in your life when you did, in fact, have exactly what you needed show up effortlessly, through perfect synchronicity and grace—times when something just came to you without any planning on your part.

A wonderful example of this was told to me by a woman in one of my classes. She recalled a time when she wanted to go on vacation but couldn't find anyone to go with her. Instead of giving up on it, she decided to go by herself. At the airport waiting to board her plane, she happened to run into an acquaintance who just happened to be going to the same place as she was, for the same length of time, even staying at the same hotel. She wound up spending her entire vacation with this acquaintance and her family, having a wonderful time and turning a superficial relationship into a lasting friendship with the whole family, which continued after the vacation was over.

See how many such experiences you can recall. Write them down if this helps you keep track of them.

STEP EIGHT

Be aware of what your thinking has been around these experiences. Do they give you confidence in your ability to call things forth effortlessly and faith that coincidence will work in your favor? Or because these things didn't come about through your effort and conscious intervention, do you tell yourself it couldn't happen again? If the latter is true for you, ask yourself, if it happened once (or multiple times), what's to stop it from happening again?

Our power to affect the world around us expands in direct correlation with our willingness to recognize the connection between our inner state and outer reality, barring nothing, the pleasant and the unpleasant. The previous two chapters addressed the connection between our inner state and the less-happy circumstances of life that we so often think of as circumstances beyond our control. If the good coincidences of life feel like circumstances beyond your control, consider reviewing these chapters with this in mind. Remind yourself that there are no circumstances beyond your control, and give some thought to what the payoffs might be for seeing yourself as powerless over the good events of life.

The material in chapters 20 and 21 is by far the most challenging in this book. Don't be discouraged if the work in them doesn't come easily. I encourage you not to succumb to the temptation to skim over the "hard part." Know that our hidden payoffs and agendas constitute some of our most profound life lessons, and that true understanding comes in stages and over years, not in a twenty-minute read. Review this material whenever life feels "hard." It will help replace the hidden payoffs we settle for because we don't believe we can have better with the happier rewards of our true heart's desires.

23

Creating Safety

A COURSE IN MIRACLES TEACHES THAT MIRACLES happen in the absence of fear, and when fear is gone, what remains is love. Fear is antithetical to love. To tap into the limitless power of unconditional love, we need to move beyond fear. In fact, our greatest safety lies in the defenselessness of unconditional love.

Of course, this is easier said than done. There's so much "real world" evidence of ever-growing dangers all around us. Loving in the face of danger seems either ridiculously naive, too saintly for normal people to accomplish, or simply insane.

In spite of the abundant physical evidence and cultural pressure to live on the defensive, there's other compelling evidence that love keeps us safer than protection. For example, Carolyn Miller in her book, *Creating Miracles,* interviewed many people who had experienced miraculous escapes from what would ordinarily be certain death or dire harm situations. Whether the situation involved driving off a cliff, maneuvering an out-of-control vehicle through oncoming traffic, or dealing with deadly attackers, many people shared a common experience just as death or attack looked inevitable. As they recognized the very worst was about to happen, instead of a fight, flight, or freeze response, they became very peaceful and calm. Fear diminished and their perspective broadened to include a concern for the others present. Those in the midst of vehicle crashes spontaneously acted to save their passengers or those in an oncoming vehicle. Those being attacked were able to step out of the victim role and show compassion and kindness to their abusers. When their perspective shifted, a miracle happened. The attacker peacefully left or the maneuver aimed at sparing the lives of other motorists turned out to save the driver as well. Through story after story, Miller offers anecdotal evidence to support her conclusion that "love without attack is the necessary and sufficient condition for miracles...." To cultivate "miracle-mindedness," she says, "means behaving like someone who is fearless, well-intentioned, innocent, and ultimately invulnerable."

Peace Pilgrim: Loving in the Face of Danger

Another inspiring example of loving in the face of danger is the late Peace Pilgrim, a remarkable woman who, in the 1950s, let go of her middle-class life, took the name Peace Pilgrim, and spent the rest of her years, until 1989, walking back and forth across the country talking to people about peace. She owned only one set of clothes and what few personal items could fit in her pockets. She ate only when she was offered food, slept indoors only when she was offered shelter, and talked to people only when they approached her first. She claimed to have no fear whatsoever, in spite of seeking out the most populated and so called "dangerous" areas to travel through on foot at all hours of day and night. She saw everyone as good and, consequently, called forth people's highest qualities and behavior.

I was fortunate enough as a young child to encounter Peace Pilgrim a couple of times as she passed through my part of the country. Hearing her speak about her life is one of the most vivid memories of my childhood. She was mesmerizing and emanated a serenity and inner peace that was contagious. Children and adults alike flocked around her.

In spite of owning nothing, living nowhere, and having no outward forms of security, she consistently experienced love, generosity, and miracles wherever she went. For her, life was a cornucopia of abundance. Peace Pilgrim became quite well-known by the time she died, and a handful of books and videos describe her, including the best-known one, *Peace Pilgrim: Her Life and Work in Her Own Words*. The following excerpt from this book is an example of how her love turned danger into safety.

> *One test happened in the middle of the night in the middle of the California desert. The traffic had just about stopped, and there wasn't a human habitation within many miles. I saw a car parked at the side of the road. The driver called to me saying, "Come on, get in and get warm." I said, "I don't ride." He said, "I'm not going anywhere, I'm just parked here." I got in. I looked at the man. He was a big, burly man—what most people would call a rough-looking individual. After we had talked a while he said, "Say, wouldn't you like to get a few winks of sleep?" And I said, "Oh, yes, I certainly would!" And I curled up and went to sleep. When I awoke I could see the man was very puzzled about something, and after we had talked for quite some time he admitted that when he had asked me to get into the car he had certainly meant me no good, adding, "When you curled up so trustingly and went to sleep, I just couldn't touch you!"*
>
> *I thanked him for the shelter and began walking away. As I looked back I saw him gazing at the heavens, and I hoped he had found God that night.*
>
> *No one walks so safely as one who walks humbly and harmlessly with great love and great faith. For such a person gets through to the good in others (and there is good in everyone), and therefore cannot be harmed.*

Listening to Inner Guidance

The state of inner safety that Peace Pilgrim so beautifully demonstrated is accessible to all of us. We all have the potential to create an aura of safety powerful enough to create an impact on the world around us. We don't need to be saints, and it doesn't require hard work so much as consistent attention. Neither is it a matter of testing our bravery by exposing ourselves to frightening situations. While Peace Pilgrim felt perfectly safe walking alone at night in the most dangerous inner-city neighborhoods, if you feel afraid of this, then don't do it! Your fear would send out a broadcast that could attract harm to you.

At the same time, if you feel perfectly relaxed and at peace in a situation that others find frightening, you don't need to increase your level of protection in response to someone else's fear. Be careful not to let others talk you into believing you aren't safe. This puts a ripple in your peace of mind, and it's your inner peace that keeps *you* safe in a situation that might be dangerous for someone else.

Learning to recognize and release the habit of fear frees us to hear inner guidance about when and where we're safe and when we're not. Peace Pilgrim was a big proponent of listening to inner guidance and doing what's sensible. Looking both ways before crossing a street, she said, is sensible—fearing streets is not necessary.

Inner guidance about our safety is always there for us when we're willing to listen. Subtle signals come to us through our thoughts and feelings that guide us to be in the right place at the right time and out of harm's way. When I lived in the Maryland countryside, I was in the habit of taking long walks along a beautiful, isolated trail far from main roads. I seldom encountered anyone other than a handful of retired people taking some midday exercise. I felt very safe there. It was a place I went for peace and solitude.

One day, from a distance, I saw a young man walking toward me on the trail. Something about him felt "wrong." The only young men I had seen here were invariably jogging, biking, or strolling with a girlfriend. This man was alone, walking slowly and unsteadily. My instincts sensed potential danger, and the "safe" thing to do would have been to turn around immediately while there was still a distance between us and head quickly back to the main road, a couple of miles back. Howe~ thought came to me clearly, telling me I would be sa I was to continue forward. I asked this guidance wh test myself this way when I felt afraid and when it w simple to just turn around. The answer I received was that if I turned around now I would never feel safe walking here again. This answer rang true so I continued. The piece of trail that was between us went under a highway, supported by a large concrete abutment. The man came to the underpass first, and I saw him slip behind the large concrete wall, out of sight. My fear escalated as I envisioned being ambushed. Still I continued, reminding myself that I would be safe. He didn't reappear, and I passed through safely, never even encountering him directly. I walked about another mile down the trail, then started back. He was nowhere to be seen on my return walk.

I came back to this place many times after that. Never did I feel afraid. I truly believe that I had been "protected" that day, and the experience of following my inner guidance left me feeling safer in the world. I was more certain that I would know in other situations when it would be appropriate to go forward in spite of my fear and when to retreat.

The Inner Experience of Safety Taps the Field

The more we simply relax and cultivate the inner experience of safety and love, the more we tap the Zero Point Field and access the unlimited power of God. This is when we see circumstances miraculously conspire in our favor, so that we truly are protected. A powerful demonstration of this happened in my own life many years ago, during a time when I was feeling particularly fearful and was working with the exercise at the end of this chapter. By the third day of practice, I noticed a real shift in my anxiety level and was feeling very peaceful and protected. That evening as I was leaving the somewhat remote country retreat center where I held a weekly class, I got a flat tire half way down the long, completely dark drive leading to the main road. In this era before cell phones, my worst fear as to be stranded in the middle of nowhere with car problems. Although I was usually the last person to leave, this time there just happened to be one group member behind me who, in a matter of minutes, changed my tire and got me back on the road. As I drove the long way to my home in the country, I was filled with a sense of gratitude that my tire had gone flat when and where it did, with help instantly available.

I was reflecting on my good fortune, feeling protected and at peace, when I suddenly felt my car wobble and klunk. The other tire had gone flat. I had an instant of panic. Here was my worst fear: on the highway in the middle of the country late at night, a flat tire and not even a spare to put on! But then I realized that I just happened to break down yards away from the only exit for miles that had a service station immediately off of it. So I continued to drive, "klunking" the short distance to the station, and left my car to be serviced the next day. Before I even had time to consider how I'd get home from there, a man who saw my situation offered me a ride. I felt intuitively that he was a Good Samaritan rather than a psycho killer, and I accepted his offer.

When I got home, I realized all of my mishaps had only added an extra thirty-five minutes to my drive. The next day, it worked out conveniently for my housemate to give me a ride to pick up my car at exactly the time I needed to go out. Through this whole experience, except for those seconds of panic on the highway, I felt peaceful, protected, and safe. What's more, I'd been meaning to get my two bald tires replaced but kept putting it off for lack of time. The thirty-five minutes it took out of my life proved to be far more efficient than the hour or two it usually took at the tire dealer. More so than if the whole thing hadn't happened, in a strange way the process of getting two flat tires on deserted roads late at night actually reinforced for me that I truly am safe. I saw that I could encounter one of my worst fears and still be completely protected.

Exercise
Creating Inner Safety

Remind yourself many times each hour of the day that you are safe. Say to yourself, silently or aloud, over and over, the words "I am safe." It's not necessary that you believe these words. "I am safe" is the belief you are creating, not necessarily the belief you hold.

From time to time, as you affirm these words, take several deep breaths, relax, and imagine a safe feeling. Let it start in your stomach as a soothing, peaceful sensation, then radiating through your entire body and slightly beyond, forming a safe, comforting cocoon around you. Feel your stomach relax into deep safety and well-being. Feel your shoulders relax as though you've just had a weight lifted from them. Imagine a hard and heavy layer of protective armor now dissolving from every part of your body because it's no longer needed.

Imagine you're naturally protected by this state of peaceful defenselessness. Picture this safety as a beautiful light of unconditional love that fills and surrounds you. See this light attracting to you everything that's for your highest good and repelling everything that's not. Also imagine this light to now be in place around you all the time, even when you're not thinking about it. Put yourself to sleep this way at night.

In moments when you cultivate this inner experience of safety very powerfully, gently radiate this comforting feeling to everyone in our network of readers, past, present, and future. Hold a heartfelt intention that we all now walk in a vibration of peace that keeps each of us safe and ripples peace to the world around us. Instead of merely being protected from the danger of the world, we are now drawing the world into a peaceful vibration with us. Picture this network of many different people in many different places and times, all joined in a peaceful light of love, and we're shining this light, powered by all of us, to every corner of the world.

24

Healing a Condition at Its Start

WHAT IF WE COULD GO BACK IN TIME to heal an illness at an earlier, less-advanced stage? Or go back even further to the moment right before an illness took hold in our bodies? Numerous researchers, Helmut Schmidt being one of the earliest, have studied the phenomenon of time displacement—that is, influencing the past—with significant positive results. Robert Jahn and Brenda Dunne found similar results. These two have produced masses of data showing that intention irrefutably can have an effect on inanimate objects. While at the time of this writing they have conducted only a relatively small number of trials to see whether intention can work backward in time, they found these time-displaced experiments to have an even greater effect.

Possibly one of the most interesting pieces of research on this was by Leonard Leibovici, an Israeli professor of internal medicine. He who conducted a controversial but impeccably controlled, randomized, and blinded experiment on 4,000 patients who had acquired sepsis while hospitalized. One group received healing prayer from a single individual who prayed for the whole group at once, while the control group didn't. The patients didn't know they were being prayed for;

even the hospital staff was unaware that a study was going on. Leibovici saw, not a small, but a major positive difference in the group being prayed for. This group showed a shorter duration of fever and an overall speedier recovery rate—even though the prayer was conducted four to ten years after their illness! The experiment used old records, not active patients, and the group of 4,000 was divided blindly into two equal groups using a random number generator so no one was aware of these patients' ultimate recovery outcomes (which at the time of the experiment, of course, were all history) until after the healing prayer had taken place.

Unfortunately for Leibovici, his intention was to show beyond a shadow of doubt the ridiculousness of applying scientific method to such alternative healing methods as prayer. He assumed people would recognize the impossibility of what the research indicated and see the study as the sham it was intended to be. Instead, many embraced it as an indication that we can indeed affect the past.

But Leibovici's is not the only research that attempted to send healing back in time. The Chiron Foundation in the Netherlands also achieved positive results when a healer sent healing back in time to rats infected with a disease.

Seed Moments

Psychologist William Braud, who has amassed the largest body of research demonstrating that human intention can affect not just inanimate objects but other living organisms, suggests that there might exist "seed" moments, perhaps at the onset of a condition, when the past is more readily changed.

The following is an experiment to go back to one such seed moment in your life to actually head off a condition before it happened. Before going into it, take some time to identify what disease you would like to address. This could be a physical or emotional condition. You could also use this experiment to "undo" a traumatic experience that left you feeling scarred.

See what feels most important and identify one condition rather than a list of complaints.

To make this experience even more effective, review the questions in step 2 of chapter 21's exercise (see page 110) to discern what gifts this condition has held for you and any payoffs that might cause you to unconsciously hold it in place rather than let it go. For example, if you're a workaholic who never slows down or lets others help you except when a health condition forces you to, your higher good might require the downtime and personal attention (even if only from paid therapists) more than release from the physical condition. Voluntarily making some difficult life choices to balance your life, without the health condition forcing you to do it, is a big step toward letting the condition go. Until you're ready to willingly incorporate healthy ways of giving yourself the "gain" of your illness, you may unconsciously hold on to it in spite of all your best healing efforts.

Be aware that, just like the person praying in the Leibovici study who sent healing back in time to many people he would never meet, there are many people sending healing back in time to you. This could be a turning point in your life if you choose it. Even if you hold doubts, feel that you haven't given your full attention to all the preceding exercises, or don't fully comprehend it all, a healing process is still taking place, powered by more than your own energy. Much of what happens in this work takes place outside of our conscious awareness. As we invoke the power of group energy to fuel our own conscious intention to grow, we set a current in motion that draws our subconscious mind into the process. Together we create a river that carries each of us, even when we're not paddling.

The more you prepare and create space for this experiment, the more you'll get out of it. For best results, do this in a quiet, reflective state of mind when you have some uninterrupted time to yourself.

Experiment
Healing a Condition at Its Start

Relax your body and quiet your thoughts with some deep, slow breaths. ❦ ❦ ❦ Let your sense of identification shift from the solidness and limitation of matter to the bright, beautiful energy that is your true essence. Through this simple shift in perception you leave behind the limitations of dense matter and start to feel your cells vibrating in light, love, and well-being. See your physical body now lit up and radiant with this energy. ❦ ❦ ❦ All the particles that make up your body are becoming less dense, with the molecules, the atoms, the subatomic particles spreading out so they can be easily reconfigured by God. As you leave the density of matter behind, you enter a realm of limitless possibilities where time and space have no bearing.

See the bright energy of other readers, past, present, and future, joining you. We are all vibrating together now, each of us bringing only higher love to the whole. As a group, we form a powerful network for healing, support, and manifestation. Take a moment to welcome these friends, and feel the light and energy of the network building. ❦ ❦ ❦

Now, picture a beautiful, shining light at your heart and at the heart of every person in our network. Imagine us—many souls, past, present, and future—sending an emanation of light from our hearts up to a giant orb located over all of our heads. Grow this energy strong and bright, a ball of pure undifferentiated healing light, to be used by each of us later in our experiment. ❦ ❦ ❦

Knowing that healing has already begun, bring to mind a condition in your life that you would like to transform. Recall back as far as you can to the early beginnings of the condition. Now travel even further back in time to when you were not just free of the dis-ease but feeling well and at peace. If you can't remember that far back, make it up in your imagination. Imagine there to be a moment in time when your soul chose to have the experience of this dis-ease or traumatic event. It wasn't a "wrong" choice; it was a way to bring certain experiences into your life. It may have helped you deepen in wisdom, strength, and compassion. It may have taught you about healing and helped you choose new priorities that would never have occurred to you otherwise. Take a moment to reflect on all that you have gained through this experience, and surround this soul choice with gratitude, acceptance, and peace.

At this point in our journey together, we know that the linear order of time is an illusion and that all time exists at once. So let us all now invoke the power of our network to help us each step out of time as we've known it. Feel the illusionary boundaries of time and space softening and melting away, allowing us to access this pivotal moment from our past in order to create the highest possible reality. All you need for this is your imagination. This new path of highest good may make a condition of dis-ease entirely disappear. It may allow you to learn the same lessons without needing to suffer in the process. It may not change anything about your condition other than allowing you to embrace and love it. You don't need to choose. Just hand it over to the wisdom of your soul and God with the intention that the highest good now manifest in a miraculous way that you may not even be able to dream of.

Once again, become aware of the orb of healing light we created earlier and the power of our entire network of minds. Imagine infusing this pivotal moment from your past with all the power and beauty of this orb. Feel God's Love completely melting through the illusion that we are anything other than whole and perfect. Let the light awaken in you the feeling of life filled with health, well-being, and joy. Let this inner experience become so vivid and real that it truly is your reality here and now. 🦋 🦋 🦋

Feel every cell in your body now vibrating with health and joy, making that feeling part of your cellular memory. Infuse the time line from the pivotal moment to the present with this vibration of health and joy. 🦋 🦋 🦋 And now, as you did in a previous exercise, send this experience of amplified health and well-being to 2 p.m.—every 2 p.m., past and future. Infuse every 2 p.m. with a reminder of this new choice your soul has made to live in health and well-being. Send it to everyone in our network of readers, past, present, and future. Imagine every 2 p.m. from now on will go off like a cellular alarm clock, reminding your cells of this new pattern of health. Realize this has already been happening all along without your knowing it because you have just sent health and well-being into your past. 🦋 🦋 🦋 Reflect on this until your mind is sufficiently boggled and then, lightly, easily let this whole experiment fly away, just as you would a butterfly that has alit on your hand for an instant.

As you come back into your body, feel your body to be refreshed, relaxed, and at ease. Don't look to see whether symptoms are still present. Observation is powerful. If we look for something long enough, we'll find it! In particular, don't immediately touch any areas of your body where you have habitually carried symptoms. This will just bring back the old cellular memories. End this experiment by forgetting about it and putting your attention on something else— preferably something pleasant.

When 2 p.m. comes along, whether you remember to pay attention or not, trust that a wave of joy and well-being is washing through you as a daily infusion of health. When you remember to notice, give thanks! Don't try to hold the moment; just feel it. Don't worry if it only lasts an instant. This instant is changing your life.

25
A Modern-Day Miracle-Maker

A MODERN-DAY MIRACLE-MAKER, one particularly dear to my heart, is the late, great healer Dr. Willard Fuller. I received my ordination under Dr. Fuller's tutelage and had the opportunity to co-lead some international healing phone conferences with him. He truly made miracles seem like the most natural thing in the world.

Though Dr. Fuller was acquainted with a number of well-known Christian evangelists, he evolved his own very different theology that embraced the truth in all religions. He spent more than forty years living a simple life as an itinerant minister, traveling around the world offering healing to anyone who wanted it. He strictly followed his inner guidance to never charge a fee for God's work, and because he wouldn't sell so much as a book, he didn't achieve the commercial super-stardom of some of his evangelical peers, though he filled auditoriums wherever he went.

Dr. Fuller's work was known for the high incidence of spontaneous healings of all varieties and magnitudes. He was particularly known, however, for the rare gift of dental healing. In his healing services many people experienced crooked teeth straightening, gum disease healing, even new teeth growing in.

And along with all kinds of dental healings, a large proportion of his audience invariably saw new fillings appear in their mouths, usually in shiny gold, silver, or porcelain. These new fillings sometimes addressed obvious healing needs, appearing where there had been severe cavities. But other times people saw their still-functional dental fillings simply change to a new substance. Dr. Fuller didn't hold the intention to fill a tooth or turn dental work gold when he worked. He simply prayed, and this was an effect. When I asked him once what he experienced when he worked, he said, "Nothing in particular, I'm just excited to see what God's going to do!"

The first healing service I ever attended with Dr. Fuller was in 1998. He was eighty-three at the time and had been conducting healing services for nearly forty years. After an hour or so of lively talk, he and his wife Dr. Althea Cook, also a minister of healing, prayed for and laid hands on everyone in the house, healing at breakneck speed. In spite of his dramatic flair for story-telling, the healing itself was done with little fanfare and no theatrics, just the briefest touch and shortest of prayers.

In stark contrast with the familiar picture of faith healers who whip their audiences into high-pitched frenzies of shaking and swooning, once healing was underway, Willard was low-keyed and his audience orderly. Afterward, he began pulling people out of their seats and quizzing them about the state of their dental work. Peering into their mouths with flashlight and dental mirror, he took a look and then let them see for themselves.

A growing buzz of excitement arose from his audience as one person after another saw either gold fillings where there had been none, or other such startling changes—nothing short of miraculous. Members of the audience rushed up to crowd around someone's open mouth to watch teeth change right before their eyes, while others inspected their own teeth with mirrors that had been passed around the room.

I enjoyed the wonder of it, feeling uplifted and inspired, but didn't realize that I, too, had received a mouthful of shiny new fillings until hours later at home when, just for the heck of it, I opened my mouth in front of a mirror. I attended many large healing services with Dr. Fuller after this, and they were always the same. After a while, the mind-blowing transmutation of teeth, as well as all sorts of other spontaneous healings, began to feel commonplace. A teenage friend of mine had the experience of all her fillings and cavities disappearing. She left the healing service with a mouthful of perfect "virgin" teeth, much to her mother's astonishment.

I travel in circles of people who are open-minded and willing to believe all manner of things most people don't. But even my most "out there" friends looked at me dubiously when I told them the story of my teeth instantly growing new fillings through prayer. I found that people who would have no trouble believing that inoperable cancer could be spontaneously healed have difficulty believing that teeth can spontaneously heal.

This is exactly why I always found Dr. Fuller's ministry of dental-healing so compelling. Teeth are such a bony, stony, unchangeable part of ourselves—a part we believe simply can't get better without the extreme interventions of drilling, pulling, filling, and replacing. If we can experience this rock-like part of our body changing so easily and instantaneously, then what, truly, is impossible? What other "carved in stone" aspects of our body, mind, and life circumstances might also be subject to some new rules of reality?

Dr. Fuller himself suggested the spontaneous occurrence of new fillings was to leave no doubt in people's minds that an act of God had occurred. Most demonstrations of healing seem vague and unprovable. They happen invisibly under the surface or with the potential for hoax, as with crutches thrown dramatically aside. A filling growing in full view of the recipient and onlookers, however, is unquestionable.

After Dr. Fuller retired from traveling, at age ninety-three, he and I held a series of phone conferences together during which hundreds of people from all over the world would call in and receive healing prayer. The results were the same. Each time there were reports of people spontaneously growing new teeth, of crooked teeth straightening, of new fillings, and other remarkable demonstrations of healing, proving that distance is no barrier to healing miracles. What's more, Dr. Fuller was very adamant that anything he can do, anyone can do, and people who attended his seminars have been known to "catch" the ability to heal teeth and other physical conditions themselves simply through opening their minds to something they had previously assumed to be impossible.

After Dr. Fuller passed away in 2009, I spent about a year teaching seminars and leading healing services with another gifted healer, a former student of Dr. Fuller's and one of those who had "caught" the gift of dental transformation. The year was a marvelous opportunity for me to witness healings of all varieties as well as this strange miracle of spontaneous dental alchemy up close and on a regular basis. During that time we saw some of our students not only receive changes to their dental work, but also pass them on to others in their healing practice.

Though many are uplifted by the phenomenon, for others it's disturbing. Some dismiss it angrily as soon as they hear about it. Others assume it to be a hoax even after witnessing it first-hand, sometimes not changing their mind until they find new gold in their own mouths. Some fear they'll get unwanted new substances in their dental work and worry, is all that metal really healthy? And still others want to micro-manage God with specific requests, as if experiencing a miracle is no different from going to the dentist and requesting a filling. Some merely ask, what's the point of all that gold?

I can't say I fully understand the mystery of dental gold. I can just share my observations that those people who came to healing services concerned about getting the "wrong" miracle or wanting only a specific miracle were more likely to leave just as they came, while those who were open and trusting experienced healing and left delighted and profoundly changed on the inside, not just in the mouth. People generally came to these events for healing to alleviate pain and illness. They left with a renewed sense of wonder, an open heart, and an awakened mind—for once we've watched gold grow right before our eyes, reality never looks quite the same. The miracle isn't just the absence of pain and dis-ease, or even the gold; it's the dawning awareness of an unlimited and omnipotent universe.

If I haven't lost you already with talk of a phenomenon that most people won't believe until they've seen it for themselves, I promise to share more of my glimmers and intuitions about it before our journey together is done. In my heart of hearts, I don't believe it to be about healing at all, nor that it requires a healer's presence to occur. I do suspect its connection to love, wonder, and transformation of the profoundest kind. I sense a deep and potent mystery to the phenomenon, and a reason why it's been put in my path. What's more, I have suspicions that you, my readers, may just be the ones to coax this mystery more fully into expression and create changes in our world that I have yet to fathom.

But, for any of you who find this glimpse into dental alchemy to be a distracting rather than compelling part of our experiment, please leave it alone, and take from this book the parts that are meant for you.

Great miracle-makers like Dr. Fuller demonstrate how fluid and unlimited reality truly is, but they're not the only pathway to miracles of this magnitude. Whereas the Tibetan monks mentioned in chapter 7 achieved miraculous mastery over the elements through a lifetime of practice, modern day firewalkers and spoon-benders gain equally miraculous mastery almost instantaneously through the energy generated in a group. We no longer need to crowd around a handful of miracle-makers. We now can simply join together and become miracle-makers in our own right.

Are you ready to be a miracle-maker of this magnitude?

Exercise
Opening your Mind to Miracles

Today, say over and over as many times as you can manage, "There are no miracles too big for God to work through me."* Say this silently to yourself, say it out loud, write it down, and post it where you'll see it. Put yourself to sleep saying it repeatedly. If it's hard to believe, say it as though you do. Imagine how it would feel to be someone like Dr. Fuller, who had absolute faith in God's power to work miracles through him. After giving your full attention to this exercise for a day, continue it for as long as you like before you move on to the next chapter's exercises.

---

*Here is another affirmation that "breaks the rules" of conventional affirmation teachings with its negative phrasing. Again, the phrasing here is deliberate. See whether it doesn't stretch your mind to start imagining what all those "too big" miracles might be.

26

Accepting the Responsibility of Miracles

IMAGINE THAT TODAY A POWER IS AWAKENED IN YOU. Not an ordinary power—a miraculous power that singles you out from other people. Imagine that you suddenly have the power to perform healing miracles. Or perhaps you suddenly develop the ability to see into the future, to see angels, or to hear messages of guidance that others can't hear. Maybe you become able to manifest things instantaneously with your thoughts. What if you now had the ability to attract an enormous flood of money and were free to use it as you please— to indulge yourself, to make a difference in the world, to create something? Perhaps you have the ability to awaken healing powers in others or to inspire and lead those around you, perhaps you have or some other undreamed power.

Take a moment to really imagine what it would be like to go to sleep tonight knowing this power is now a part of who you are. Can you sleep? Are you burdened, excited, grateful, afraid? Imagine waking up with this big power. How do you go about your life? Do you do what you normally do, or does everything change? What do you tell your friends? How does it feel to live with this power? Does it challenge the limits of

ve you can—or should—be, do, or have? Would
ably shake your trust in reality? Does your ego run
his power so that you feel elevated above others, or
ve you more humble than before? Is your stronger
on to help others, to show off what you can do, or to
hide ɔ. e way you're now different? How does it change you,
change your life, change people's expectations of you? Do you
feel more connected to other people or more separated? More at
peace or more conflicted? Does it feel like a gift or a burden?

The Fear of Miracles

Miraculous shifts take us beyond the realm of the familiar,
beyond what we fully understand. They can be overwhelming
and, along with (or instead of) rejoicing, we can find ourselves
contracting in fear. It starts as an inflow of new energy, perhaps
taking the form of healing, a financial windfall (lottery winners
are notorious for having trouble managing their sudden
wealth), the awakening of a spiritual gift, or an ecstatic spiritual
experience. It becomes an uncomfortable overload when we
find that we can't turn it off at will and go back, even for brief
moments, to the comfortable familiarity of life as we knew it.

Well known pioneers of the human potential movement, Stanislav
and Christina Grof, have identified a whole syndrome related to
energy overload, which they've named "spiritual emergencies."
Signs of a spiritual emergency may include an ecstatic and
overwhelming experience of God or a too-much-energy feeling,
and may be accompanied by a variety of physical symptoms.
Spiritual emergencies may also involve the sudden awakening
of intuitive gifts, such as clairvoyance or clairaudience (seeing or
hearing aspects of nonphysical reality), or out-of-body experiences
in which conscious awareness separates from the physical body.
A person may have a sharpened intuitive knowledge of things
without any physical way of knowing them.*

---

*For more on this, see Stanislav and Christina Grof's book, *Spiritual Emergency*.
Also, on my website, I have an article, "Making Sense of Spiritual Emergencies" for
bringing energy-surge experiences down to earth.

Most of us never have to deal with the problems of "spiritual emergencies" in which we feel like an energy spigot has been turned on with no way to turn it off. A more common problem is the unconscious programming that keeps our energy spigots so tightly controlled we unknowingly shut down the flow of God energy long before it can become overwhelmingly profuse.

We generally don't realize we're afraid of miracles until they're upon us. I know an extremely competent healer who not only does excellent work on other people but has healed himself of terminal heart disease, diabetes, and a number of other physical complaints, including dental issues. This healer received training from the master dental healer Dr. Willard Fuller and had no doubt that all things are possible. He decided he was going to grow back his missing tooth and, because of his work with Dr. Fuller and his own personal track record with healing, he thought this would be easy to do. He set about healing himself, as he had on many other occasions, and soon experienced a very pronounced cracking sensation in his jaw, in the area of the missing tooth. As he recognized these tangible signs of his healing intent manifesting, his instinctive, first response was a big, fearful "NOOOO!" which immediately stopped the crackling. Needless to say, he didn't grow a new tooth that day. He was surprised by his own response to what he assumed to be healing in progress, and he took it as a sign that he still had work to do in stretching his mind open to the limitlessness of healing.

There are a number of reasons we clamp down on anything beyond what we're use to, including miracles. We may have personal issues of worthiness—ingrained beliefs that we don't deserve so much. Or fearful expectations that if we have more, we'll just be that much more disappointed when we lose it. This is where it's helpful to again review the information and exercises of chapters 20 and 21 to discern what unconscious, limiting expectation of life we are perpetuating or what payoff is present through limitation.

Another reason we may shut down rather than embrace miracles is due to how mind-boggling they are. Our mind tries to make sense of something that often can't be processed through the filters of what we already know. Then we start doubting and questioning our own perceptions: "Did that really happen?" It's disorienting to have reality as we've known it thrown into question, and we wonder "What is real?" Then the fear that we're losing control takes over, and we grasp all the more tightly to what's familiar. We may experience a crisis of identity: "Who am I if all I thought I knew for certain isn't true?" All this takes place in the blink of an eye, nipping miracles in the bud before we even know what happened. Becoming aware of this instinctive resistance helps slow it down and gives us opportunities to consciously choose rather than automatically react.

The Morphic Field of Disbelief

I've filled this book with so many references to science and research because of the huge role science has played in shaping our subconscious expectations and beliefs. Anyone who has sought alternative health treatments against medical advice, even after careful research and with full confidence in their choices, may still find it to be a frightening and lonely road simply because there is such a strong collective energy field of belief—a morphic field (refer back to chapter 2 for more on "morphic fields")—that "Doctors know best." It can be a difficult energy field to go up against and still maintain peace of mind. For those making such choices with their health, it becomes very important to the success of treatment to stay immersed in the energy of those who have faith in it and to stay away from those who don't. Although some areas of the world are still infused with miracle-friendly spiritual traditions where miracles are accepted, expected, and regularly appear, the United States isn't one of those areas. Science and even many of our spiritual traditions have, for the most part, eradicated miracles from the collective mental air waves—until recently, that is. New science is starting to provide a doorway through which miracles may re-enter. Science is making sense of miracles. The more rational miracles seem, the less our rational minds will interfere with them, and the more we will look for and find miracles.

Yet there is a responsibility that comes with miracles, which is another reason we may subconsciously repel them. Miracles are a manifestation of tapping the limitless energy of God, or the Field, whichever you choose to name it. Energy is a form of power, and with power comes the responsibility of making a bigger mark on the world. Having such energy makes living the role of hapless victim with no power over external circumstances increasingly difficult. Even if we perceive the miracle itself to be a circumstance beyond our control, the event of the miracle has left us with greater resources than we had before. If we have a miraculous healing, for example, we go from having the depleted capability of an ill person to the greater ability of a well person. Suddenly we have more choices to make, and people may expect more from us. Miracles change us so that we can't help but have a bigger impact on the world around us for better or worse, which can feel like a burden if it's unfamiliar or unwanted.

One last pitfall of miracles I'll mention here is what the ego can do with them. The ego only believes in the reality we can fathom with our physical senses. It operates from a place of fear and tries to control the external environment to maintain order and safety.

As we experience in a big way going beyond the confines of our ego, which we do when we open to God energy, our ego automatically responds protectively to restore order and control by bringing things back into the realm of the familiar. This is normal. We can expect to have ego reactions of one sort or another following big God experiences. We just don't have to take them seriously.

Typically when we have a powerful God experience, the ego's response is some combination of "I'm weird" and "I'm special." The "I'm weird" voice tells us we're crazy, no one will believe us, maybe we shouldn't believe ourselves, we're different (and separate) from everyone else, there's something wrong with us, and other such suggestions. The "I'm special" voice tells us we're more evolved than others, we are specially chosen, specially gifted, elevated, and know more.

Paradoxically, these two go hand in hand. A person will probably be more aware of one of these voices than the other, but the opposing voice will be whispering in the background. The dark side of feeling "specially chosen" is a fearful awareness of responsibility and aloneness. Along with the disconcerting feeling of being "weird," invariably somewhere lies a deep-down pride in having a "special" condition. The kernel of truth in the "delusion" of being specially chosen is that we *are* specially chosen for an important spiritual mission only we can do. This awareness ceases to be delusional when we recognize that *everyone* has been specially chosen for their own unique missions.

Exercise
Imagine Yourself a Miracle-Maker

As you were invited to do at the opening of this chapter, spend a day imagining how it would feel to live with a miraculous power. What if you suddenly developed the power to perform healing miracles? Or to see or hear things that others can't? What if you could manifest things instantaneously with your thoughts? Or had the ability to attract an enormous flood of money and were free to use it as you please? Perhaps you have the ability to awaken healing powers in others, or to inspire and lead those around you, or some other undreamed power....

Let your reflections give you insight into your comfort level with being a miracle-maker and your readiness for it. As you do today's exercise continue to remind yourself that, "There is no miracle too big for God to work through me."

Questions for Thought

What magnitude of miraculous power would feel like too much for you to receive? What magnitude of power would

- boggle your mind and upset your belief systems?

- uncomfortably challenge the limits of what you believe you can or should receive or the limits of who you believe you are?

- create burdensome or frightening new responsibilities?

- cause you to feel separate and alone?

27

Becoming
a Miracle-Maker

WE ARE NOW ENTERING A NEW PHASE of our experimental collaboration. This is where we move from the realm of manifesting miraculous results to making a miraculous difference in the world. We will take a step into the responsibility of power. The next experiment raises our capacity to receive, hold, and disseminate God energy. It will help rewire us individually so we may access and accept more energy. This not only enables us to be more effective in all areas of our lives, but it also makes us more effective conduits for serving the world around us.

We also will give attention in this experiment to awakening a specific spiritual power of our choosing. By *spiritual powers* I mean such qualitative states of being as love, faith, courage, acceptance, grace, peace, joy, living in the moment, compassion, honesty, gratitude, integrity, forgiveness, vision, wisdom, creativity, surrender, trust, receptivity, and generosity, to name only a few.

Awakening spiritual power is very different from manifesting a specific outcome. A power confers the capacity to manifest many outcomes. For example, the disappearance of a physical symptom is an outcome, whereas the capacity to heal is a spiritual power. Awakening the power to heal promotes a state of health more broadly than does simply making a particular illness disappear. Creating a circumstance or event that evokes joyfulness is another example of an outcome, while the pure experience of joy, regardless of outer circumstances, is a spiritual power. The magnetism of inner-generated joyfulness has a way of attracting to us a multitude of opportunities, circumstances, and fortunate experiences, and it even enables us to find the blessing in experiences that others would see as misfortunes.

I've purposefully used the word *awakening* rather than *manifesting* in relation to spiritual power because stepping into true God power is always a process of becoming more fully who we are. Any spiritual power we could possible want is already within us just waiting for us to use it.

Awakening power can be accomplished simply through the slightest act of intention and may offer little evidence, immediately, that anything at all is different. Yet this intentional willingness to become more fully our True Self opens the door for God's Will to override our plans, taking us in directions we may never have anticipated. What began imperceptibly takes on a life of its own and may change us dramatically, sometimes in ways that feel unexpected and out of control since our ego is no longer leading the way. Yet the journey is always in the direction of our highest good and highest joy. It's like getting on a roller coaster that starts out slow and safe, then suddenly the *real* ride begins. We're completely out of control, and there's nothing we can do but hold on for dear life, surrender to the ride, and wonder what made us get on in the first place. Before we know it, though, the ride's over and we remember why we got on—for the fun of it! And no matter how out of control we felt, we recognize afterward we were safe the whole time. Maybe we will even turn around and buy another ticket! So, if you choose to continue with the next few experiments, understand the power of the process you're setting in motion. Whether it feels rattling or like the best fun you've ever had has a great deal to do with how ready you are to embrace change. Either way, get ready for the ride of your life!

The spiritual power you choose to awaken is entirely up to you. Why give attention to just one aspect of spiritual power when, in truth, we already have all power? Why not awaken more than one or many powers at once? There is no cookbook formula for this, and each of you must listen to your own inner guidance around this work. I suggest just one simply because choosing many is often the ego's way of choosing none. Choosing everything can be a way of committing to nothing, and this awakening of power is in essence an act of commitment. Plus, awakening a spiritual power invariably requires giving up some lesser one. And here lies the real work of stepping into True Power.

These lesser powers are those rooted in fear that we've grasped as a substitute for True Power because we believe we can't have better. A lesser power is the satisfaction of being right that we cling to when the Power of Love eludes us. Or it could be the sympathy and other payoffs of being a victim that we settle for when we fear we won't succeed at creating a better life. It might be the power of invisibility we opt for when we believe we'd fail or be rejected if we took the spotlight and let ourselves be seen. Or the power that illness gives us to ask for what we need, set limits, and change our priorities—things we wouldn't dare do without dis-ease or illness forcing us to—that we may unconsciously choose over the power to heal. It's the power of being an underdog when we fear the expectations others would have of us if we embraced our power to lead.

Recognizing the lesser power you're most attached to may help you see clearly the spiritual power you're most ready to awaken. Or it may be the other way around. If you know what power you most want to experience more fully, consider how your life could change if you were to become truly powerful in this way.

What new responsibilities would come with it? What options would you lose? What expectations would other people have of you? Being willing to acknowledge and release the payoffs of powerlessness is a necessary step into power.

Before continuing on into this next experiment, take some time to identify what spiritual power you would most like to awaken and experience fully in your life. When you give this power a name, write it down somewhere, put it away to refer back to in about a year, at which time you can review all the ways it has actualized. Also identify the lesser power most holding you back (victim consciousness, invisibility, being right, etc.). What commitment are you willing to make to releasing this lesser power?

A term I've heard used since the early days of the New Age movement decades ago is "Light Worker." It's been so overused and trivialized that I haven't used it in many years. Yet it aptly defines our next step. To consciously work with the Light and Love energy of God means accepting the responsibility of power. It's not possible to be a Light Worker and still embrace the payoffs of victim consciousness. We can't be Light Workers and not accept responsibility for whatever scarcity, limitations, and dis-ease keep us small. Neither are we Light Workers if we have out-of-control egos more intent on showing off our gifts than helping others find theirs. In fact, the most authentic Light Workers I've encountered through the years would never dream of identifying themselves as such. They don't preach; they simply have a way of leaving others feeling more at peace and better about themselves. So if you're ready, let's step onto the path of becoming a Light Worker.

As our experiments become lengthier and have more far-reaching implications, it's especially important to set aside quiet time for yourself to experience them. The more you prepare yourself and your space for this step, the more life-changing it will be.

Experiment
An Initiation into Power

Relax your body and quiet your thoughts with some deep, slow breaths. ❦ ❦ ❦

Once again, let your sense of identification shift from "particle" reality to "wave" reality. You may notice that each time you do this it becomes a little easier. Feel your physical body becoming soft, relaxed, and weightless. ❦ ❦ ❦ Feel the particles that make up your physical body begin to gently vibrate and spread apart, leaving more and more space in between. God fills the space in between. Soon even those wide-spaced particles melt into the Light of God, and what was once dense matter is now a beautiful wave of light energy, free of all the laws that limit matter. Take a moment to simply be in the energy of Light and Love, recognizing that God is everywhere; there is no place God isn't. ❦ ❦ ❦

Now see the network of other readers, past, present, and future, with you, all vibrating together in the Light and Love of God. Together we amplify the energy of Light and Love exponentially. Take a moment to feel the God energy of the network building. ❦ ❦ ❦

Picture the light of our network to be so bright that it attracts to us an even greater light. Imagine this as a brilliant spiritual sun shining its light on all of us. Know this to be the Light of Divine Love and feel it to be profoundly peaceful. Let it wash through you, melting away anything that has dimmed the radiance of your own inner light. Invite it to rewire your energy circuits so that you can now assimilate and disseminate a larger flow of God energy. This increased light energy enables you to more easily move beyond life's struggles into joy and productivity, and it empowers you to serve the world around you in a bigger way. Take a moment to let the light change you. Open your mind to any messages or insights that come to you about this new step into power. ❦ ❦ ❦

As you're filled with the deep peace of Divine Light and Love, you now are more powerfully radiant than you were before. Send a ray of light to each person in our network of readers. Let your light join with theirs to assist in their transformation and growth. As you do this, recognize that everyone in this network is doing the same for you, and together we help one another to gently rise into our spiritual power, easily, each at our own pace, in our own way, and with no need to feel overwhelmed by it. ❦ ❦ ❦

Imagine that we are joined by a myriad spiritual beings—angelic helpers, spiritual guides, beings of Light and Love—who assist in the spiritual evolution of humanity and of our planet. Call upon any names of God that are meaningful to you, and feel their presence adding light to our network. Know that these beings have gathered with us to facilitate an initiation into power for all those ready to take a bigger role in the work of Love and Light. See our network of readers arranging into a circle of light, a beautiful circle of souls. Our spiritual guides are now preparing a place in the center of the circle where the initiation will occur.

In a moment you will have an opportunity to move into the center and claim the spiritual power that you are ready to awaken. This initiation into power is a gift that each of us earns through our willingness to trust God and honor God's Will. Our spiritual helpers applaud our willingness to join them as Light Workers on the planet and offer an added gift, one that we don't need to earn. This is the gift of Divine Grace. Grace is a blessing you may never have thought to ask for, yet it satisfies the deepest longings of your soul. It's an unconditional gift that you don't need to earn or deserve, an expression of how loved you are by something you can't see.

It may feel and manifest differently for each who receives it. Be open to receiving this and other blessings beyond anything you've dreamed.

When the time feels right, imagine yourself moving from your place in the circle to the center. Take a moment to just be in the center with the spiritual guides, and notice what you see and feel. You may sense or see spiritual beings with you. Experience every spiritual being radiating a powerful vibration of love to you, helping to awaken in you your chosen power. Say with strong intention, silently or out loud, "I now claim my power of...." Fill yourself with the inner experience of the power you've chosen. Vividly see it, feel it, do it, and be it in your imagination.

Fill yourself so completely with the energy of this power that it can't help but overflow. Send it to everyone in the circle around you. Send it as light, energy, emotion, and vibration to anyone in your life you'd like to give the gift of this power to. ❦ ❦ ❦ Send it to the world as a healing emanation.

When your initiation feels complete, take another moment to be still and receive the gift of Divine Grace. Imagine the most beautiful vibration of love holding you like a Divine Mother and giving you the most precious gift you've ever received. You don't need to know how this blessing will manifest in your life. Just let it in. Just let it be. ❦ ❦ ❦

Now ask for a sign—something you're sure to see in your life from time to time, and when you do, it will be a reminder to release your lesser power and to give, in an unconditional act of service, the spiritual power you've just claimed. ❦ ❦ ❦

When you're ready, imagine yourself moving out of the center and retaking your place in the circle, becoming a helper to other souls who are stepping in for their awakening into power.

Take a moment to let the ritual complete in your mind's eye. Let your attention shift to your body, the physical space around you, and the ground beneath you. Take a couple of deep breaths to bring yourself all the way back.

Exercise
Keep Your Power Growing

To follow up this initiation, know that the best way to keep your new power is to give it away. During the coming week, find as many opportunities to give your power in unconditional service as you can. Find a way to give this power away at least once a day for at least a week.

18
Shining the Light

O NE OF THE MOST SELF-SERVING THINGS we can do is to shine our light outward in some way—to make the world brighter by our presence. The purely personal benefits of doing unconditional good are many. It's well-known that the best therapy for just about anything is often stepping out of ourselves to help another. Along these lines, Dean Ornish, who compiled extensive research on the connection between love and health in his book *Love and Survival*, writes, "What is also important in a number of studies is not only how much [love] you *get* but also how much you *give*." He went on to cite a particular study of more than seven hundred elderly adults that showed, "the effects of aging had more to do with what they contributed to their social support network than what they received from it. The more love and support they offered, the more they benefited themselves."

Offering a bit of light to the world around us may actually keep us younger and healthier. And it doesn't require grand gestures to be meaningful. Acts that don't try to save the world but simply demonstrate a faith in goodness may be just what help us all believe the world is worth saving.

Through the years I've encountered many spiritual teachers and leaders of social change. A number stick in my mind as

.cially powerful. However, along with the movers and .akers who are working in obvious ways to heal the world, other people have moved me just as deeply in spite of their humble settings and activities. One such person is a woman I used to regularly encounter when I bought gas. She worked in a small glass booth between gas pumps on a busy city street in a neighborhood considered rough. Her job certainly wasn't glamorous, easy, or overtly aimed at world healing. Yet she had an aura about her. Her smile was authentic and heartfelt whether it was to a polite elderly person or an intoxicated troublesome person. She seemed to create a ripple of peace around her in this chaotic atmosphere. More than once my encounter with her changed my day significantly for the better. It's hard to know how profoundly she affects her world through these simple emanations of love. My guess is that her impact has been considerable.

There was also a man who held the lowly job of collecting shopping carts outside a big supermarket. He had a smile and a word for everyone who walked in or out, got to know an astonishing number of people by name, and often broke into operatic renditions of popular tunes as he helped people with their bags. His poor reading and writing skills made it hard for him to qualify for the indoor job of bagging that he wanted, but I never saw him any way but cheerful—no, *cheerful* is too small a word. The man seemed to make it his job to extend kindness unconditionally to everyone. His work on that parking lot was nothing less than a ministry and, decades later, I still remember him profoundly. In a busy urban parking lot plagued with crime, who knows how great an effect he had on his world?

More recently, I heard someone tell a story of being at a restaurant with her mother and when it came time to pay the check, their waitperson told them someone at another table had paid their bill. Their benefactor had already left by then and they never did find out who did it or why. But I could tell that it was a gift that will remain fondly in their memories for years to come.

Many of us celebrate holidays and special occasions by exchanging piles of gifts. If you've been the giver or receiver of such mountains of material things, how many of them are remembered ten years later? What have you done recently, or ever, to make yourself deeply memorable, in a good way, to people who barely know you?

Questions for Thought

1. What are some small acts of kindness that have left a lasting impression on you?

2. What small act could you imagine doing that might be remembered for years to come by the recipients?

3. What small act would take little from you and would give you a lift by doing it? In other words, forget about what you should do or what would look good, forget about heroic efforts and sacrifices meant to impress, and consider what would just plain feel good to do. When you think of something that fits this description, you may well have found the gift that someone will be remembering decades after the event. How can this not be an important contribution to the world?

Exercise

Now Do It

Do something kind that will be remembered for years.

29

A Return to Our Heart's Desires

LET'S RETURN TO OUR OWN PERSONAL HEART'S DESIRES again. Remember many chapters ago when you wrote that list? This time, however, we'll approach manifesting work as a Light Worker. Light Workers recognize there truly is no difference between one's own highest good and that of others. This doesn't mean it's better to give than to receive. It literally means there is no difference because there is no separation. As we act in service to our personal well-being, we become more empowered to serve the world, and as we serve the world, we naturally attract all that we need to thrive.

Rather than bringing a whole list of desires to this experiment as we did in a previous experiment, the focus here is to discern what you want *most*. This isn't because we can only manifest one thing at a time—it's because where we have passion, we have creative energy, and our strongest desires are often nudges in the right direction. I think of it like a line of standing dominoes. Where we have the greatest passion is the first domino, and when we tap it over, it takes all the others with it. So take a moment to bring to mind something you want more than anything.

Now let yourself start to feel a sense of pleasant anticipation around your desired outcome. Happy anticipation is a form of Love energy and, consequently, it is very magnetic to our highest good. It's important to understand the difference, however, between pleasant anticipation and attachment. Attachment is rooted in fear: fear that we won't get what we want, fear that we won't like it unless it's just so, fear that it won't happen unless we micromanage every step. Attachment keeps our attention focused in the future so we're not present to the joy of the moment. Happy anticipation is rooted in love and keeps us more fully present because we're happy, not worried, about what's to come. Anticipation is a feeling of being full in the moment, whereas attachment is one of waiting—and hoping—to feel full in the future.

In the example I shared in chapter 12 of manifesting a new home, the imagining I did was light and unattached: "Wouldn't it be lovely!" as opposed to "I'll just die if I don't get this!" or "I never get what I want!" I enjoyed my fantasies and they left me feeling full rather than fraught with angst over what I couldn't have. This is the energy and power of positive anticipation.

If you don't have enthusiasm for something, it won't be easy to create it. If you're lacking a feeling of passion around what you've picked as your highest heart's desire, it could mean you've chosen what you think you *should* want as opposed to what sparks the most feeling. You may have picked an in-between step, as in "I'm now manifesting a lot of money so I can buy a new home" as opposed to what you really want: "I'm now living in my perfect home!"

Sharing your dreams with supportive others can help you stay enthusiastic and positive. Be careful, though, not to talk about your manifesting work with people likely to "rain on your parade." Doubt, fear, and worry are catching!

Do the following experiment in a quiet, reflective state of mind when you have some uninterrupted time to yourself.

Experiment

Giving and Receiving Are the Same

Relax your body and quiet your thoughts with some deep, slow breaths. 🦋 🦋 🦋 Imagine the clear, bright energy of other readers, past, present, and future, joining you. We are all vibrating together now in shared consciousness beyond the illusionary limits of space and time, each of us bringing only higher love to the whole. See this joining as beautiful, sacred, awe-inspiring, and filled with the potent energy of love.

As a group, we form a powerful network for manifestation and miracles. Recognize how much more powerful we are together. Our joined intentions heighten our magnetism to our highest good. Together, anything is possible. Take a moment to feel the light and energy of the network building. 🦋 🦋 🦋

Now bring to mind your highest heart's desire. Bring it to mind lightly, playfully, as one of many possible outcomes that could please you. Picture it as having already happened and enjoy walking around in this reality. 🦋 🦋 🦋

Turn this reality over to God in perfect trust that this or something better is now materializing in your life. Let it fly away as easily as a butterfly from your hand, and picture not one but countless butterflies taking flight as readers in all places and times lightly let go with you. 🦋 🦋 🦋

Imagine us all joining in a common intent that all readers now manifest their deepest hearts' desires, possibly in the forms they imagine, but just as possibly in forms better than they yet know how to name. You may find it easier to imagine others manifesting miracles than to imagine yourself. Know that you don't have to have absolute faith or belief, because there's now a whole group of people supplying the faith in you that you may not yet have in yourself.

Now we're going to expand our access to the manifesting energy of the Zero Point Field—to God energy—through love. Allow someone to come to mind—someone whose highest good you would like to support. See who pops into mind before you have a chance to think about it too hard. Trust that this is the right person. This person is going to further your highest good by offering you an opportunity to open your heart unconditionally.

Letting go of all agendas about what you think this person should do, simply send your deepest heartfelt desire that this individual now receive his or her highest good. Don't give it a form. Let go of your personality's investment so that you simply fill their spiritual bank account without any stipulations on how they spend it. Unconditional love is a powerful spiritual gift that is always received whether we ever fully comprehend it through the filter of our personality. Give it unconditionally with faith that your gift will be received and used in the way this person most needs. See the person's perfection, beauty, Higher Self. Imagine yourself loving this person the way God loves her or him, with complete acceptance. 🦋 🦋 🦋

End by sending your gratitude to this person. This soul has just helped you tap the limitless manifesting power of God by providing an opportunity to love. See this person fade into the Loving Light of God, and let this miracle experiment go.

Imagine that your miracle has already manifested, that you just don't know where in time and space it has been placed. It's like a birthday present in the mail. You know it's there, you know it's yours, and you know you'll receive it simply by going about your life with as much contentment and pleasure as possible.

Exercise
Practice Giving

This week, instead of giving attention to waiting and looking for your heart's desire to manifest, give attention to supporting the highest good of others. Consider doing one or all of the following:

1. Just as you did in the preceding experiment, let someone come to mind. It may be the same person, someone different or more than one person. See where your love just naturally wants to go, and find a way to give unconditionally, with no agendas around how your gifts are received, used, or reciprocated. You can give quietly and anonymously through prayer, or you can take more outward action. Listen within to what feels right. You'll know it's "right" when the giving itself feels to be a joyous miracle.

2. This week, recognize that everyone you encounter has had moments of darkness and could be right now in the midst of a dark night of the soul without you even realizing it. Know that the light of your love could make an important difference in someone finding a way out of darkness. Shine your light unconditionally as a free gift, with no judgment about the recipient's condition and no expectations about how they use your gift of love. The most powerful way to help someone change is to let go of wanting them to change and, instead, authentically accept them as they are. Truly, the way to turn darkness into light for someone is with love devoid of our ego's opinions about how they should be and what they should do. This week, practice shining your loving acceptance freely.

3. Dedicate yourself for a day to praying for the highest good of one particular reader. You don't know who it is; you simply send it to one soul in our whole network of readers, past, present, and future, trusting that your gift

will find its mark. For one day, let this unseen person's highest good be as important to you as your own. You may get some intuitive impressions of this person you're praying for, but it's not necessary. Imagine that someone may be doing the same for you.

30

Taking a Quantum Leap

"It's the end of the world as we know it..."

FROM THE SONG TITLE, R.E.M.

The true consequence of miracles is that they change us. They don't just remove a symptom or change an out-come so that we can keep living the same life in the same old way, with just a little less inconvenience. In an instant, life never looks the same again. Miracles have the potential to bring about "the end of the world as we know it" and start us on a journey of Self. Well-known author and mythologist Joseph Campbell calls this the "hero's journey" and describes it as "...a mystery of transfiguration—a rite, or moment, of spiritual passage, which, when complete, amounts to a dying and a birth. The familiar life horizon has been outgrown; the old concepts, ideals, and emotional patterns no longer fit; the time for the passing of a threshold is at hand."

Physicist and author of *Taking the Quantum Leap,* Fred Alan Wolf, likens this shift in being to a "quantum leap" and writes, "taking the quantum leap means taking a risk, going off into uncharted territory with no guide to follow. Such a venture is an uncertain affair at best. It also means risking something that no one else would dare risk."

As uncertain and risky as it seems, paradoxically, this type of leap requires less effort, less pain, and struggle than everything else we've tried to date. It is, however, something completely different. It means acting outside of our lifelong conditioning, stretching our imagination to places it has never been before, surrendering where we usually exercise control, and most of all going bravely into the unknown. This last miracle experiment is an invitation to take not just a step but a quantum leap into true empowerment, knowing that in doing so life will never be the same.

The Mystery of Spontaneous Dental Transformation

Before we plunge in, let me set the stage a bit. I've mentioned here the remarkable work of Dr. Willard Fuller and other healing practitioners whose practices includes the spontaneous effect of dental transformation. While these healers have lumped this phenomenon into the general category of "healing," I've seen people's fillings change to shiny new metal without any obvious healing of a condition, and I've seen others who have a physical healing without the accompaniment of new fillings. I've also encountered many remarkable healers who achieve dramatic results in their work without ever manifesting this dental phenomenon. For years I've wondered, what's the meaning of the dental bling?

The more I've pondered it, the less I believe it to be simply a manifestation of the reparative energy of healing. To a large extent, the practice of healing operates within the reality paradigm of problem-solving. This is true whether it's in the context of conventional medicine, faith healing, or energetic healing. Many healers and virtually all of their recipients start with a problem and then set about fixing it. Healers need the reality of illness to practice their craft. Consequently, there's a way that the very practice of healing perpetuates the reality of illness—even when the problematic symptom is successfully resolved, even when it's resolved instantaneously and miraculously. Some New Thought spiritual paths don't even recognize the practice of healing because of this and instead give attention to the reality of wholeness, calling dis-ease an illusion. Think of it this way: winning a battle every day on behalf of peace and goodness, from now until the end of time, won't create peace. It will only perpetuate war. Paradoxically, in a very real way, healing keeps illness alive.

While it remains a mystery to me that I don't claim to fully understand, I suspect the dental alchemy is less about healing and more about awakening—awakening from the illusionary paradigm of illness and healing to the greater spiritual reality of wholeness. I also believe this manifestation of new fillings to be a sign that significant, quantum leap-like life changes are in the making. Whereas healing makes symptoms disappear, leaving the recipients as good as they were before the illness, the dental gold and silver signals a dizzying leap into the kind of passage that Joseph Campbell and Fred Alan Wolf speak of in which, as Campbell describes, "the old concepts, ideals, and emotional patterns no longer fit."

So why does this energy of awakening affect teeth? I've long studied the language of symptoms and know that the body speaks to us in very literal metaphors. People with sore backs typically feel unsupported; those with sore hands are often trying to handle too much by themselves; people with heart problems are likely to be broken-hearted or have lost their zest for life. Teeth are a particularly rigid, unchanging part of the body and a good physical representation of all the hard, unbending structures of life—including our belief constructs. When we speak metaphorically of the need to "chew on" something, we mean we need to think about it; we need to break it down, process it, and then assimilate it. For those who witness it, the spontaneous occurrence of new dental fillings is so fantastic that they can't help but expand their thinking about what's possible. Previously unbending beliefs change instantaneously. It not only gives us something radically different to "chew on"—it gives us something new, literally, to chew with!

Channeling the "Golden Transmission"

My insight into the true significance of these dental miracles came to me all at once as an "Aha!" kind of revelation. It was, and still is, purely intuitive. My only proof has been my own private test. When I had this flash of awareness, I asked God for a sign. I asked that if this phenomenon is truly an energy transmission of awakening rather than a healing and signifies that an opportunity is at hand for quantum leaps in growth, then I wanted to send it successfully to my husband—who was in another city at the time.* The sign I was looking for was that he experience a change in his fillings and some corresponding manifestation in his life.

This felt like the right sign for a couple of reasons, one being that my husband had been longing to see his fillings change ever since his first healing phone conference with Dr. Fuller. He checked his teeth frequently—and consequently was very familiar with his dental work—but never found the slightest change.

The other reason is I wasn't a person who sent "transmissions." It was out of my comfort zone. Up to that point, I had never even attempted to channel whatever energy it is that results in gold and silver fillings. In the events I co-led with my healer colleague, who is truly expert at relieving pain and physical disability, I was far more comfortable supporting his healing work by "priming the group" than in laying hands on others myself.

When I even thought of it my ego ran wild with simultaneous fears that I wasn't capable and fears that I was. I worried that my real work of empowering individuals and teaching the strength we have together would be undermined if I suddenly started turning teeth to gold. I've always eschewed the role of guru. I dread the inevitable projections and dependency that I've seen follow the best of healers, no matter how hard they protest that it's all coming from God, not from them. At the same time, I

---

*I don't recommend sending a specific, results-oriented energy transmission to anyone without his or her permission because it crosses ethical boundaries. However, I have blanket permission from my husband around such things.

envied the easy audiences that these special miracle-makers drew. Working side by side with them, I often felt like I was trying to sell broccoli next to the ice cream vendor.

Yet here I was, sending an energy transmission to my husband, demanding proof of my revelation in the most unlikely-to-be-confirmed form I could imagine, all but daring God to prove me wrong.

As soon as I sent this energy—which in my revelation was identified as a "Golden Transmission," a golden light that goes in through the third eye chakra in the middle of the forehead but requires an open, loving heart in order to "take"—I called home and left an urgent message: "Bill! Check your teeth!"

Busy schedules kept us from talking for more than a day, by which time Bill had discovered shiny new silver in all his fillings and had experienced some wonderful serendipitous events related to his work as a musician. A dental appointment a couple of weeks later confirmed that, even though he previously had a combination of newer and older dental work of differing substances, he currently had very uniform silver fillings that all appeared to have been installed at the same time.

Interestingly, the experience I had of receiving new dental work myself as well as this experience of "passing" it to someone else both came when I needed it, at what turned out to be life-changing moments, not as a result of my ego wanting it or not wanting it. In observing my own experiences and those of others, "wanting" seems to have nothing to do with this phenomenon.

An Experiment That's Never Been Done

Is my insight about the "Golden Transmission" truth or fiction? I admit, even I don't know for sure except for the reality of Bill's dental work and my sign of confirmation showing up just as I asked it to. Now is when you need to listen to your own intuition and guidance. If you're game—and here is where only the hardcore believers need step forward—let's undertake an experiment that's never been done.* It's a step out of my comfort zone, which has often been a signal to me that something extraordinary is about to happen!

For those of you who've read this book from the beginning, you've had a lot of practice in being miracle-minded, which will make our next experiment all the more powerful. For those of you who like to read the ending first, you may have a different sort of advantage in being unattached to the outcome and not trying so hard to make it work.

What can all of you personally expect? Be open to no less than the fulfillment of your dreams. Just don't expect anything expected. This isn't about setting a predictable process in motion. This is where "The familiar life horizon has been outgrown; the old concepts, ideals, and emotional patterns no longer fit; the time for the passing of a threshold is at hand," as Joseph Campbell put it.

This threshold leads to dreams you never thought to dream before, things your heart has always longed for but your mind has never known how to name, and these may require you to leave predictability far behind, "going off into uncharted territory with no guide to follow. Such a venture is an uncertain affair at best. It also means risking something that no one else would dare risk," as Fred Allen Wolf says.

But then again, as R.E.M tells it, "It's the end of the world as we know it (and I feel fine)." You just may find that the end of the world as you knew it is the best thing that ever happened to you. You also may come away with some shiny new dental work but, of course, if you're waiting and watching too hard for the bling, you're bound to miss it. Remember calling the wild miracle that won't come until you stop hunting, stop watching, stop waiting, and just settle into enjoying life.

---

*It has already been done, of course, because of the illusionary nature of linear time. A more accurate truth is that just as everything has already happened, so is everything happening for the first time. As I wrote these words, this experiment had the freshness of the unknown. Let it be that for you, too.

I make it a rule never to ask others to take any bold steps that I wouldn't take myself, so let's make this leap together!

This is our longest and most significant experiment. Let your preparation and approach to it reflect the transformation you'd like it to seed in your life.

Experiment
The Leap

Relax your body and quiet your thoughts with some deep, slow breaths. 🦋 🦋 🦋 Let your sense of identification shift so that instead of feeling yourself to be defined by your physical body, separate and dense, you become aware of yourself as clear, bright, beautiful energy. Through this simple shift in perception you leave behind the limitations of dense matter and start to vibrate in the unlimited way of light, energy, and love. Feel the very cells of your physical body becoming less dense, the molecules, the atoms, the subatomic particles spreading out, vibrating in love and light. You're shifting from the limited paradigm of "particle" reality to the limitlessness of "wave" reality.

See the bright energy of other readers, past, present, and future, joining you. We are all vibrating together now in joined consciousness beyond the illusionary limits of space and time, each of us bringing only higher love to the whole. Take a moment to experience the light and energy of the network building. 🦋 🦋 🦋

Now bring to mind the human part of you that can so easily get caught up in the ups and downs of life. Know that all these human experiences are polishing your soul in ways your personality may never comprehend, and give thanks for the richness of your life, even with its messiness and challenges. At the same time, recognize that no matter how immersed you may at times feel in the dramas of your life, you can always step back from them all and, in an instant, return home to your True Self.

Do this now by reaching up for help. Know that spiritual assistance is always there when we reach for it, and as you do, you can feel a force gently lifting you out of the limited reality of your earthly life. You're not taken away, just given a lift, and you instantly feel more at peace as you step back from human emotion. You may literally feel physically lighter as this shift happens. You become infused with the unconditional love that is your natural state and you can now look upon your human self and life experiences with greater love, acceptance, and gratitude.

As you awaken to the expanded reality of your Higher Self, your heart wants only to radiate love to the world around you, and you find yourself joined by many helpful nonphysical beings of Love and Light who assist in the evolution of humanity and of our planet. Make this more powerful and personal by calling upon God and the forces of Light and Love using whatever name(s) are meaningful to you. Feel them adding light to our network and increasing our power to help.

Ask these beings of Light and Love—true Light Workers— to show you the world as they see it. Where you see hopelessness and despair, ask to be shown the wholeness that is always present even in the midst of strife. Ask these spiritual helpers to show you the world as it could be—as it is becoming—a vision of peace on earth and well-being for all. 🦋 🦋 🦋

Join these Light Workers in their mission by radiating the pure Light of faith, compassion, acceptance, and peace to the world. 🦋 🦋 🦋 This may be as far as you take our last experiment. The next step is optional. If this is your stopping point, for as long as you like simply be with the beings of Light and Love, joining their ranks as a Light Worker by offering light to our world. When you're ready to finish your meditation time, thank the Light Workers for their help.

Thank all the souls in our network of readers who have been quietly with you on this journey. 🦋 🦋 🦋 Last, but not least, love, accept, and honor yourself as purely and completely as God does. You are worth it.

If you're called to go further, imagine a threshold now coming into view. But before you move through it, stop and just be still. You can see me on the other side waiting for you. I will give you the most gentle touch on the forehead to pop, like a soap bubble, your last resistance to God energy so this wondrous transmission of golden light can flood through you. Crossing the threshold isn't a step you need to take now.

The "step" isn't impatient for us. Each of us has our own path and timing—sometimes to sit at the threshold and take stock is exactly the right thing to do. It's important to listen to your own wisdom regarding this because the power of group spiritual work here is profound. As we hold the intention in the context of this network of Light Workers to fully claim our true power and highest good, it may happen more quickly than we expect. It may never be possible to live our ordinary lives again. We may receive the gift of suddenly needing to act where we had been comfortably passive. We may be blessed with the ability to see ourselves so clearly that we can no longer honestly claim the role of victim. We may have the divine wisdom come upon us to know that we've outgrown circumstances of our lives even before we're clear about what will replace them. We may grow a new inability to be who others want us to be and in any number of ways be forced out of comfortable familiarity.

So simply stand at the threshold for this moment. Behind me there is a spiritual helper, one of the Light Workers, waiting to be a special guide to you in the next part of your journey. This Guide will wear whatever face you need it to. Look and see who's there. Your Guide is filled with love for you and will help smooth and illuminate your path so that life lessons can now be learned through joy rather than struggle.

Fully experience this moment between worlds—the life that's safely familiar, the unknown journey ahead filled with new joys that may land you far out of your comfort zone. The Guide of your next step won't intervene until you've chosen to cross the threshold. This moment is for you alone to decide. 🦋 🦋 🦋

If you decide to stay where you are, recognize this to be a powerful place of taking stock before moving on. Your spiritual work is to practice self-love, for when you truly find compassion and acceptance for who you are, for where you are, and for all that's been, you'll be ready to take the next step.

If you choose to cross the threshold, taking the first step of the Hero's Journey, do so now and feel a rush of God energy filling you, body, mind, and spirit. I meet you with a gentle touch to the forehead that sends a soft, golden light rippling all through you. Something in you has changed and will never be the same. Your Guide steps forward to welcome and honor you.

There's nothing more to do. Your journey will find you, as will your miracles. It's no longer yours to know how or when or what; your intentional step has surrendered your ego's plan to a higher plan. Feel yourself now bathed in a golden light, and take a moment to be with your new Guide who may have something to give you, show you, tell you, or offer you for the journey ahead. Just take it in, surrender, and know you can trust the process of life. 🦋 🦋 🦋

When the experience feels complete, let it go, but know your Guide will remain with you, as will many loving souls who have been with you through all of our experiments. Take some deep breaths to bring yourself back to a normal waking state. Stretch to help you feel back into your body. Come back feeling refreshed, peaceful, and with the absolute knowing that life is good!

———•———

Thank you for sharing this journey with me, and God bless you!

With Love,
Lynn Woodland

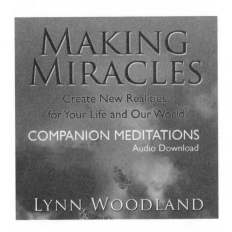

www.namastepublishing.com

These companion meditations feature the author guiding you through nine of the book's experiments. These beautiful readings are enhanced by the music of consciousness and sound design expert Carlos A. Boyce Jr., along with Bill "Butch r" Baker, to move you into a deep meditative state.

Carlos Boyce, aka "Songdoctor," appears courtesy of Blue Rose Records.

An Invitation

Dear Reader,

Creating a new path, through joining together, to all we ever dreamed and more is the purpose of the Miracle Experiment. This book, *Making Miracles*, is meant to bring groups together in community across time and space, and in person. I urge you to share the exercises in this book with others. Find a group, start a group, or simply read this book with a friend. Miracles are best when they are shared!

A suggested study guide for *Making Miracles* is available on Namaste Publishing's website at www.namastepublishing.com. I invite you to use this guide if you find it helpful. However, there are as many ways to structure a group as there are groups, so don't be afraid to be creative, make use of the wisdom of your members, and let what you start take on a life of its own.

You might consider registering a *Making Miracles* study group in your area on MeetUp.com as one way of connecting with others interested in participating. In addition, there is a forum on Namaste's website dedicated to *Making Miracles* and the Miracle Experiment. Namaste Publishing and I invite you to share with other readers, through this forum, the miracles you see happening in your life. You will also be able to post responses to others who share their miracles, as well.

Blessings,

Lynn Woodland

About the Author

Dr. Lynn Woodland has worked at the experimental edges of the Mind/Body/Spirit, Transpersonal Psychology, and New Thought movements since 1972. She has taught workshops on the metaphysical principles of healing and manifestation for decades, blending science, spirituality, psychology, and practical application to help students produce striking results in amazingly short periods of time. Her particular area of interest and expertise is in what gives rise to miraculous experiences.

Her background includes twelve years as a chemical dependency and mental health counselor. She has studied and practiced Therapeutic Touch, Reiki, and other forms of energy and spiritual healing since 1981. In 1983 she helped found and directed the Baltimore Center for Attitudinal Healing, a free health crisis resource center for people dealing with life-challenging illnesses. During this time she specialized in mind-body counseling for individuals and groups. In 1987, Dr. Woodland left the Center to lead classes and workshops based on her own work regarding practical spirituality and expanding the limits of reality as we know it.

She also trained with the late world-renowned faith healer, Dr. Willard Fuller. She received her ordination in 1998, and later her Doctorate of Ministry, through Dr. Fuller's Lively Stones Fellowship. From 2008-9 she collaborated with Dr. Fuller on a series of international phone conference healings. She has operated a variety of online and in-person healing ministries since 1999.

cly, Dr. Woodland is the creator of The Miracles ww.QuantumSpiritUnlimited.com), a year-long . of online spiritual education leading to ordination, ⸱ is the founder of Miracles of the Spirit Ministry (ww ᵥ..MiraclesoftheSpirit.org). Her first book, *Power, Effectiveness, and Spirit,* won two awards from the Midwestern Independent Publishers Association. To learn more about Lynn Woodland's work, visit www.lynnwoodland.com.

Suggested Reading

Campbell, Joseph. *The Hero with a Thousand Faces*. Princeton: Princeton University Press, 1949.

Dossey, Larry, MD. *Healing Words*. New York: HarperCollins, 1993.

Dulchinos, Donald. *Neurosphere*. York Beach: Red Wheel/Weiser, LLC, 2005.

Friends of Peace Pilgrim, *Peace Pilgrim, Her Life and Work in her Own Words*. Santa Fe: Ocean Tree Books, 1982.

Grof, Christina, and Stanislav Grof, M.D. *Spiritual Emergency*. New York: Penguin Putnam, 1989.

Grof, Christina, and Stanislav Grof, M.D. *The Stormy Search for Self*. New York: Penguin Putnam, 1990.

Hawking, Stephen. *Black Holes and Baby Universes and Other Essays*. New York: Bantam Books, 1993.

Jampolsky, Gerald, M.D. *Love is Letting Go of Fear*. Berkeley: Celestial Arts, 1979.

Jampolsky, Gerald, M.D. *Teach Only Love*. New York: Bantam Books, 1983.

McTaggart, Lynne. *The Field*. New York: HarperCollins, 2002.

McTaggart, Lynne. *The Intention Experiment*. New York: Simon & Schuster, 2007.

Miller, Carolyn. *Creating Miracles*. Tiburon: H. J. Kramer, 1995.

Morse, Melvin, M.D., and Paul Perry. *Closer to the Light*. New York: Villard Books, 1990.

Morse, Melvin, M.D., and Paul Perry. *Transformed by the Light*. New York: Ivy Books, 1992.

Morse, Melvin, M.D., Paul Perry. *Where God Lives*. New York: HarperCollins, 2000.

Ornish, Dean, M.D. *Love and Survival*. New York: HarperCollins, 1997.

Pritchett, Price. *you2*. Dallas, Texas: Pritchett and Associates, Inc., 1990.

Schrödinger, Erwin. *What is Life? and Mind and Matter*. London: Cambridge University Press, 1969.

Shucman, Helen. *A Course in Miracles*. Mill Valley: Foundation for Inner Peace, 1975.

Wolf, Fred Alan. *Taking the Quantum Leap*. San Francisco: Harper & Row, 1981.

namaste
PUBLISHING

books that change your life

Our Service Territory Expands

Since introducing Eckhart Tolle to the world with *The Power of Now* in 1997 (and later with *Stillness Speaks, A New Earth*, and *Milton's Secret*), NAMASTE PUBLISHING has been committed to bringing forward only the most evolutionary and transformational publications that acknowledge and encourage us to awaken to who we truly are: spiritual beings of inestimable value and creative power.

In our commitment to expand our driving purpose—indeed, to redefine it—we have created a new website like no other. We are creating a global spiritual gathering place to support and nurture ongoing individual and collective evolution in consciousness.

As a member of the Namaste Spiritual Community online, you will have access to our publications in a variety of formats, plus supporting resources found exclusively on our site. The live discussion groups will center around a variety of topics including spirituality, health, and relationships, as well as our most popular titles. You will have access to Namaste authors through their blogs, discussion forums, and a myriad of multimedia content. And because we are all teachers and learners, you will have the opportunity to meet other members and share your thoughts, update and share your "spiritual status," and contribute to our interactive online spiritual dictionary.

Here you will also find the wisdom of Bizah, a lovable student of Zen, dished up in daily and weekly doses. And rich content from our authors' and publisher's blogs, as well as timely guidance found in our daily Compassionate Eye blog.

What better way to come to experience the reality and benefits of our Oneness than by gathering in spiritual community. Tap into the exponential power to create a more conscious and loving world when two or more gather with this same noble intention.

We request the honor of your presence at
www.namastepublishing.com

Have you been noticing more frequent serendipities?

Do you feel on the verge of something?

You may have already sent these experiences back through time to yourself by reading this book!